CONFUCIANISM

Ch'u Chai

Professor of Chinese Culture and
Philosopher, retired

Winberg Chai

Chairman of the
Department of Asian Studies
City University of New York

Barron's Educational Series, Inc.
Woodbury, New York

All inquiries should be addressed to:
Barron's Educational Series, Inc.
113 Crossways Park Drive
Woodbury, New York 11797

Library of Congress Catalog Card No. 73-3977

Paper Edition
International Standard Book No. 0-8120-0303-9

PRINTED IN THE UNITED STATES OF AMERICA

Table of Contents

This book is designed to serve college students, as well as general readers, as a handbook of Confucianism, in regard to its origin, its development, its great exponents, and its success in dominating Chinese thought for the last twenty-five centuries.

An introductory discussion characterizes Confucianism in Chinese history and a brief account is given of the Confucian classics.

The body of the book consists of nine chapters, in chronological and historical sequences, each being devoted to a major exponent or phase of the Confucian school. In addition, each chapter is preceded by a general survey dealing with the background against which the Confucian thinker developed his version and ideas of what Confucius taught. We also give biographical sketches of the leading exponents concerned and a critical commentary of their writings and doctrines.

For convenience, references are commonly given to translations of Chinese texts, but the original Chinese has been consulted. We regret that the high cost of printing the Chinese makes it impossible to add here a bibliography of the Chinese works that we have used.

Because this subject is a large and complex one, it is not possible to include all the important exponents and thinkers of the Confucian school within the cover of a single volume. Who should be selected and who rejected requires critical consideration. In making the choice, we wish to acknowledge much valuable assistance and criticism freely rendered to us by many kind friends who wish to remain anonymous.

We should also like to thank Professor Leonard R. N. Ashley of Brooklyn College for his editorial assistance and Dr. Vincent F. Hopper of Barron's Educational Series, Inc. for his appreciation of the need for this book. Full acknowledgment is made in the footnotes of references to other authors, as well as many of the pioneers whose translations of Chinese works. have made our task easier. Their names can be found in the bibliography.

We are especially indebted to Mr. Henry W. Chai for his assistance in typing the manuscript and in checking references.

C. C.

W. C.

New York City

Confucianism
in Chinese History

The *Ju* philosophy is known in Western literature as Confucianism because it had its beginning in the teachings of Confucius (551–479 B.C.), founder of the *Ju* school. The name of Confucius had seldom been used in China in connection with his school. The word *ju* literally means "*literatus*" or "scholar," one well versed in the six arts;[1] ceremonials and music (including poetry), history (or writing) and numbers, archery and charioteering. In the *Lun Yü* (*Analects* VI–11), "The Master, speaking to Tzu Hsia, said: 'Be you a noble *ju*, not a lowly *ju*.' " Here the word *ju* had a wider implication. Anyway, the *ju* had been so closely identified with the Sage that the use of the word *ju* was restricted exclusively to the Confucian school, distinguishing it from other schools of thought.

The *Ju* philosophy has long been dominant in Chinese thought. The place which it has occupied in Chinese history has been comparable to that of religion in other countries. All educated Chinese have been trained in accordance with the *Ju* philosophy. The *Four Books*, which consist of the *Lun Yü*, the *Mang Tzu*, the *Ta Hsüah* (*Great Learning*), and the *Chung Yung* (*Doctrine of the Mean*), have been the holy scriptures of the Chinese people. It is in the *Ju* philosophy that they live,

1

move, and have their spiritual being. It is no exaggeration to say that China is the land of Confucianism, the *Ju* philosophy permeating the Chinese mentality and outlook of life.

The question often arises whether Confucianism is a religion. Confucianism, as is generally asserted, is not a religion, for it has no religious structure or sanction. It presents lofty intellectual ideals, but there is nothing to be feared by one who fails to live up to them. In competing with a religion that preaches the assurance of immortality, Confucianism suffers from its silence about the realm beyond life. Moreover, Confucianism attaches great importance to humanity and stays fairly close to ethical and political considerations. Nevertheless, Confucianism, though not a religion, is religious in some of its features. There has been reverence for *T'ien* (Heaven), which is assumed to throw its weight on the side of the virtuous. There have been ceremonial and sacrificial practices, considered to be essential to the welfare of men. There has been belief in moral order and values, which involve a concern for the whole humanity, its suffering and its well-being. Even more important, there have been noble ethical teachings, which have permeated Chinese life in all its aspects, whether moral, political, or social. This is how the Chinese people derive religious comfort from Confucianism.

In spite of some religious aspects, Confucianism remains to this day a philosophy and a system of ethics. Even as an ethical or philosophical system it has undergone many changes due to interpretation and alien influences. We shall undertake, first, to trace the various stages of its development; second, to show main ideological trends with which it had come into contact; and third, to appraise the significance and effects of its dominance in Chinese thought.

The place of Confucianism in Chinese history, though always influential, has varied considerably from one period to another. The evolution of Confucianism may be briefly traced in the following periods.

Historically speaking, the Eastern-Chou period (771–255 B.C.) was one of intense political, social, and intellectual activity during which all established conventions and institutions underwent fundamental changes. The impact of these changes on man's mind gave rise to an "Era of Hundred Philosophers," to which China is indebted for her intellectual heritage. In terms of significant influence upon Chinese thought, there are four main systems of Chinese philosophy: Confucianism, Taoism, Mohism, and Legalism. The major schools of philosophy can be characterized as man-centered and world-centered and preoccupied in seeking to establish a better world. They all originated between the sixth and third centuries B.C. when old institutions and order had lost their value. Each of them can best be considered in terms of its approach to pressing problems presented by current political and social chaos. For instance, Confucius, as a great humanist and historically minded, proclaimed himself "a transmitter and not a creator, a believer in and lover of antiquity" (*Lun Yü*, VII–1). What he transmitted was the Chou culture.[2] He based his teachings on the authority of ancient sage kings and the orthodox feudal concepts of the Chou period, from which he evolved his ethico-political system of a paternal government, on the basis of the doctrine of *jen* (human-heartedness).

In contrast to Confucius' humanism, which stressed social order and an active life, Lao Tzu (c. sixth century B.C.) taught the Taoist philosophy that is essentially naturalistic and anti-social. As a believer in naturalism, he attributed all human miseries to man's own folly; he urged the people to lead a life of "naturalistic simplicity and tranquility," in accordance with the Taoist doctrine of *wu-wei* (no action contrary to nature). It is obvious that the only principle of government consistent with the Taoist doctrine of *wu-wei* is that of "*laissez-faire*," with the minimum of organization and regulations.

Another eminent thinker of the Chou period was Mo Tzu (Mo Ti, *fl.* 479–438 B.C.), founder of the Mohist school. He disapproved of both the Taoist "primitive society" and Confucian "elaborate rites." To counter the influence of Confucius and Lao Tzu, he advocated a theory for the organization of an ideal human society upon the great principle of "all-embracing love" to secure world peace and prosperity. Recognizing the weakness of man, he contrived to embody this great principle in a Supreme Being in Heaven and a monarchical sovereign on earth.

These three schools of thought competed for supremacy, though none of them was accepted as orthodox. In each of these schools the teachings of the founder were amplified by disciples or followers. Mencius (372–289 B.C.) and Hsün Tzu (*fl.* 298–238 B.C.), for example, elaborated the Confucian teachings, while Ch'uang Tzu (*fl.* 369–286 B.C.) elaborated the Taoist teachings. However, among the disciples of Hsün Tzu, Han Fei Tzu (d. 233 B.C.), the chief exponent of the Legalist school, made his influence felt in the third century B.C., during the transition from the Chou feudal system to the Ch'in empire (221–207 B.C.). The Legalists, as typified by Han Fei Tzu, stood for firm and autocratic—even totalitarian government and for stringent laws as the framework of social order. Thus they came into conflict with Confucian scholars in particular and most of the earlier thinkers such as Taoists and Mohists in general.

This conflict was in a large measure responsible for the notorious edict of 213 B.C., issued by the Ch'in emperor Shih Huang Ti at the instigation of his Legalist minister, Li Ssu (d. 208 B.C.), another disciple of Hsün Tzu, ordering the destruction of the ancient classics, especially the books of the Confucian school. As a result of this edict, the intellectual activity of the Classical Age or the Age of the Hundred Philosophers came to an abrupt end.

Confucianism is commonly considered to have triumphed over its rivals in the second century B.C., when the imperial system had been consolidated under the Han rulers. While agreeing with the Ch'in's basic goal of homogeneity, the succeeding Han dynasty (206 B.C.–220 A.D.) disapproved of harsh measures such as those taken by the Ch'in emperor. Then Tung Chung-shu (*c.* 179–104 B.C.), the greatest of the early Han scholars, proposed to the emperor that unity be sought by new means—by the elevation of Confucianism at the expense of the other schools of thought.

But the Confucianism expounded by Tung Chung-shu and adopted in the early Han period was something quite different from that originally set forth by Confucius and his immediate followers. Han Confucianism was in fact tinged with ideas from rival schools, especially Taoism. Mohism had not survived the Ch'in suppression, and Legalism had fallen into disrepute, even though elements of its political theory lingered in the thinking of the ruling class. Taoism, however, had become influential in government circles to the extent that its *wu-wei* doctrine was adopted as state policy and its occultism became an often-held personal creed. This fact determined the general character of Han Confucianism.

Generally speaking, the Han scholars divided themselves into two groups: the "New Script" school and the "Old Script" school. Their textual disagreement was accentuated by a difference in their views about the true significance of Confucius and Confucianism. The Han scholars of the New Script school were rich in religious faith. On the basis of the apocryphal literature which grew up within the New Script school, the Confucian partisans attempted to deify Confucius and to transform Confucianism into a religion. This absurdity of the New Script school, more than anything else, was responsible for its ultimate decline in the second half of the Han period. Meanwhile, the influence of Taoism spread, together with that of Buddhism, which had been introduced from India in the first century A.D., or even earlier. Chinese philosophy blossomed anew as a result.

From the third to the tenth centuries of our era, Chinese civilization gradually felt the influence of foreign cultures. The philosophical thought can be represented by the Taoist metaphysics (known as the *hsüan hsüeh* in Chinese, literally "mysterious learning") of the Wei Tsin period (220–420 A.D.), and Buddhism of the Sui (581–618 A.D.) and T'ang (618–907 A.D.) dynasties, which had little connection with politics but exercised a great influence on Chinese thought. During the period Buddhism flourished in China and, in collaboration with Taoism, overshadowed Confucianism. Indeed, Buddhist scriptures, translated into Chinese, grew to vast proportions, and Buddhist temples and monks increased so rapidly that they had to be checked by imperial decree in 845. In the meantime, Buddhism was beginning to undergo a great transformation, obscuring its Indian origin and developing into Chinese Buddhism as the Chinese philosophers evolved teachings of their own to modify and adapt the alien creed. One sect of Chinese Buddhism was the Meditation sect or *Ch'an*, better known to us by its Japanese name *Zen* (the Sanskrit *dhyāna*). Its discipline of meditation and emphasis on the mind undoubtedly contributed to the rise of Neo-Confucianism of the Sung (960–1278) and Ming (1368–1644) periods.

The rise of Neo-Confucianism marks the turning of Chinese intellectuals away from Buddhism and back to Confucianism. This new movement, which can be traced to the T'ang dynasty, developed under the Sung dynasty and reached its climax in the Ming dynasty. This new system of philosophy, which dominated Chinese thought for more than seven hundred years, was brought about by Confucian thinkers who were well versed in the Buddhist and Taoist ideologies. Hence Neo-Confucianism incorporated into Confucian ethics and politics Buddhist cosmology and Taoist metaphysics, just as Han Confucianism had absorbed the teachings of its rivals to survive in that period. This synthesis of thought, as attempted by these Neo-Confucian philosophers, constituted a major contribution to Chinese philosophy.

There was, however, considerable diversity in Neo-Confucian thought, but two main trends predominated: the rationalistic and the idealistic. By the Chinese the former is called the *Li* (Principle) *Hsüeh* school, and the latter the *Hsin* (Mind) *Hsüeh* school. The Rationalistic Neo-Confucianism is nearer to the whole rationale of Confucian thought, and the Idealistic Neo-Confucianism is more akin to the thought of *Ch'an* Buddhism. These two schools differ widely in ideology and methodology. Their ideological controversy on major philosophical problems evoked great interest in their day. In any event, the significance of Neo-Confucianism lies in its effort to revitalize Confucianism with new elements of Taoism and Buddhism, as it was in danger of becoming stagnant. As a result of this infusion, there was a renaissance of the Confucian thought; it regained its strong hold on the intellectual life of the Chinese and held firm until the opening of China to the West.

Lastly, the intellectual trend of the period from the Ch'ing dynasty (1644–1911) to that of the Republic (1911 to the present) may be characterized by two major forces: the revolt against Neo-Confucianism and the impact of the West. The Ch'ing scholars, like those of the Han period, took no interest in abstract thinking and placed emphasis on action. It was natural to expect that they would launch an attack on the metaphysical learnings of the Sung thinkers (*Sung Hsüeh*). In protest, they styled themselves "followers of the Han Learning (*Han Hsüeh*)," to show that they sought to "purge" Confucianism of the Buddhist and Taoist elements which the Sung thinkers had incorporated into it. The *Han Hsüeh* scholars have been considered to be the most skeptical and critical thinkers that China has produced. But although their critical outlook can be classified as a school of pragmatism, it is still not a school of philosophy. The emphasis has been all too much upon linguistic study and textual criticism and far too little upon genuine philosophical enquiry. Perhaps in time, penetrating criticism of this pragmatic movement itself may result in a legitimate new school of philosophical thought.

The so-called New Culture Movement of the 1920's was a later manifestation of this critical spirit. Taking the positivism and pragmatism of the West as their inspiration, and science, social progress, and democracy as their chief objectives, the leaders of this movement identified Confucianism with the old regime and everything in the past that, to their minds, had interfered with new ideas and forces of progress. Their rallying cry became "Down with Confucius and his company!" But the time-tested Confucian ideals could not be put aside so easily, and a controversy arose that still rages, unfortunately, to the present day.

We need not here review the pros and cons of the anti-Confucian movement. Our subject is Confucianism itself. In ethics, Confucianism upholds the five "constant virtues" of *jen* (human-heartedness), *yi* (righteousness), *li* (propriety), *chih* (wisdom), and *hsin* (sincerity or good faith); in politics, it stresses the moral importance of human relationships. In its last analysis, virtue alone constitutes the ultimate goal of man. These Confucian principles and values, in which we can still find an inexhaustible store of wisdom and a useful set of rules for right living, could readily lead to the modern concepts of human rights and political democracy, however much, in the course of time, Confucianism has suffered in the hands of politicians and emperors who stressed that aspect of Confucianism which supports the autocratic rule.[3] For two thousand years Confucianism had been closely affiliated with the imperial system, not as an immanent principle but as an ideological tool of imperial rulers to maintain political stability. There is some justification, therefore, for the contention of Chu Hsi (1130–1200) that "the way of Confucius had not been put into practice for a single day" during the centuries of imperial rule.[4]

With the entire fabric of Chinese society shaken and shapes of things to come so uncertain, it is still too early to conclude the history of Confucianism. For the last two thousand years Confucianism has dominated Chinese thought and moulded the national character. It has also given continuity to the old civilization of China which, far from becoming extinct in its development, showed a vitality in its struggle for survival and supremacy. The significance of Confucianism lies in its moderation, harmony, and synthesis, its "spirit of human reasonableness,"[5] or a sort of golden mean (*chung yung*). There may still be hope that this spirit will have an "ameliorating effect on Communist materialism and atheism."[6]

Above all, Confucianism is a blend of idealism and realism. It is metaphysical and ethical. It attaches importance to spiritual cultivation and yet has a deep concern for the ordering of the world. It has a vast scope and a great depth, and yet appears to be simple and direct. It has a flexibility and versatility, and yet forms a single thread of unity—one main tradition, one main stream of thought—always having as its goal a particular kind of highest life. This kind of highest life is "not divorced from daily regular activities," and yet at the same time "it goes straight to what is beyond the Heaven." [7] The first part of this expression represents the *Tao* of man and the second part, the *Tao* of Heaven. As the *Tao* of man, it is concerned with human affairs; as the *Tao* of Heaven, it reaches for the sublime, the transcendental. In Confucianism, the man who attains to this kind of highest life is called the "Sage," or the "Great Man." What is more significant lies in the fact that although the sphere in which the "Sage" or the "Great Man" lives is a transcendental one, his achievements are in the main concerned with the business of the world. This is the great teaching of Confucianism.

It is the spirit of synthesis that must be borne in mind, if Confucianism is to be understood.

The Classics of the Confucian Tradition

Let us now turn to the Confucian Classics (*Ching*) which, together with the commentaries, constitute the first of the traditional four categories of Chinese literature, the other three being *Shih* (History), *Tzu* (Philosophers' Writings), and *Chi* (Miscellany). *Ching* and *Tzu*, in fact, were originally not much differentiated. Only after the Ch'in ban on the ancient philosophical and historical works was formally lifted by the Han emperor (191 B.C.) were the scholars able to undertake the task of gathering and arranging the fragments of the ancient works which had been scattered among the people. It was in this manner that the *Shih* (Poetry), the *Shu* (Documents or History), and the *Ch'un Ch'iu* (Spring and Autumn Annals) were once more rescued from oblivion, and *I* (Change), as work of divination, having previously escaped the "Ch'in's fire." These four Confucian texts, together with the *Li Chi* (Book of Rites), constitute the *Wu Ching* (Five Classics), traditionally accepted by the Chinese as the written cultural heritage of ancient China. The only loss, so far as the Confucian classics were concerned, was the *Yüeh* (Music); only one chapter survives in the Works of Hsün Tzu, an exponent of the teachings of Confucius and a critic of Mencius.[8]

Shu Ching or *Book of History*

The earliest Chinese work of historical fragments preserved today is the *Shu Ching*, the *Book of History* or the *Book of Documents*, containing a number of political documents of ancient dynasties, arranged in four historical periods: (1) *Yü Shu*, Documents of Yü Shun (2255?–2205? B.C.); (2) *Hsia Shu*, Documents of the Hsia Dynasty (2205?–1766? B.C.); (3) *Shang Shu*, Documents of the Shang Dynasty (1766?–1122? B.C.); and (4) *Chou Shu*, Documents of the Chou Dynasty (1122?–628 B.C.).[9] Thus these documents cover a period of seventeen centuries, with considerable *lacunae*. They were fragmentary, and we know little of how they were compiled and transmitted. There are two important texts, the old and the new. The old text contains many documents forged by later scholars, while the new text is comparatively authentic; but even the authentic documents were most probably written during the Western Chou period (between the eleventh and sixth century B.C.). The various forgeries, which have led to endless philosophical and philological controversy during the past twenty centuries, are beyond the scope of the present discussion.

The content of the *Shu Ching* may be said to fall into three main groups: (1) *Tien* (Canon) and *Shih* (Oath), which include accounts of historical facts concerning ancient kings as well as their public orations; (2) *Kao* (Proclamation) and *Moa* (Declaration), which are official ordinances and edicts on specific subjects; and (3) *Shun* (Instructions), which are philosophical expositions of general principles of government. All these documents are permeated with religious ideas and didactic passages. Despite their political purposes, these documents are also literature and were written with a great deal of rhetorical effectiveness and literary charm. All important state papers of the subsequent periods adopted literary phrases and political expressions from these documents so that they had a continuing influence on literature and life in China.

Shih Ching or *Book of Poetry*

The *Shih Ching*, the *Book of Poetry* or the *Book of Songs*, is the earliest anthology of Chinese poetry. It is a collection of popular poems and folk songs, dating from the beginning of the Chou period to the seventh century B.C. When and how these poems and songs were first collected and arranged we cannot know for certain. According to one early tradition, Confucius selected 311 out of more than three thousand poems and set them to music, but the "Ch'in fire" (213 B.C.) resulted in the loss of six poems. Modern scholarship, however, has vigorously argued against the traditional view. It seems to us that if Confucius did not edit the *Shih Ching*, he did refer to the *Three Hundred Poems* on more than one occasion in the *Lun Yu*, thus suggesting that the number of poems had been fixed during, perhaps even before, his time. The book was originally called the *Shih*. In the Han dynasty it was designated as one of the Five Classics (*Wu Ching*), under the title of the *Shih Ching*. The texts were considerably altered during the *Mao, Han, Lu,* and *Ch'i* editions of the Han era. The current text is that of the traditionally accepted *Mao* edition, containing 305 poems and totaling 39,244 characters.

The book is divided (according to the type of music to which the words are set) into three sections: *feng* or popular songs, *ya* or courtly odes, and *sung* or sacrificial and temple hymns. Some later scholars analyzed and classified them into three types: *fu* or narration, *pi* or comparison, and *hsing* or association. In the *Shih Ching*, there are some poems and songs of the *fu* type, clearly narrative, which may be called the prototypes of narrative poems in classical literature. *Pi* and *hsing* are often mentioned together as *pi-hsing*, and many poems and songs in the book are of the two types, noted for the use of simile and metaphor and the practice of starting a poem or a song by evoking images quite apart from the central subject. As a matter of fact, these three types—*fu, pi*, and *hsing*—merely concern the form of the *Shih*, and have nothing to do with content; they have been employed for many centuries as rhetorical devices in folk songs.

These pieces comprised the basic instruction Confucius offered his students in poetry. His reasons for teaching poetry were several. During the period it was customary in polite society to illustrate conversation with verses. Thus, Confucius was led to remark: "Without studying the poems, one will have no hold on words." (*Lun Yü*, XVI–13). Apart from this, however, Confucius stressed the moral value of the poems and summed up the benefits of studying them as follows:

> Poetry evokes inspiration and leads to introspection; it contributes to one's sociability and liberates one's frustration. In the study of poetry, one learns to serve one's parents and prince; besides, one is better acquainted with the names of birds, beasts, weeds and trees (*Ibid.*, VII–9).

I Ching or *Book of Changes*

Another important book which existed before Confucius is *I Ching*, the *Book of Changes*, which was referred to merely as *I* or *Chou I*. It was originally a manual of divination, based on the eight simple trigrams, from which evolved a fanciful system of philosophy. By means of the eight trigrams, the Chinese sages grasped the mysteries of the universe and tried to show the people how to avoid misfortune and to take advantage of opportunities. According to the *I Ching*, there is the Supreme

Ultimate (*Tai Chi*), out of which, the Two Modes (*Yi*) are produced and designated by the *Yang* (——) and the *Yin* (— —). Through the Two Modes, there arise the Four Symbols (*Hsiang*):

⚌ The *Yang* in its major   ⚏ The *Yin* in its major
⚍ and minor phases   ⚎ and minor phases

Through the Four Modes, there arise the Eight Trigrams (*Kua*), each made up of combinations of three broken or unbroken lines:

☰ *Ch'ien* (1)   ☷ *K'un* (2)   ☳ *CHEN* (3)

☲ *Li* (4)   ☱ *Tui* (5)   ☴ *Sun* (6)

☵ *K'an* (7)   ☶ *Ken* (8)

These original Eight Trigrams did not have philosophical significance, however, until the Ten Appendices were added to them, and subsequently these Eight Trigrams were extended to Sixty-four Hexagrams. Each hexagram was supposed to be the symbolic representation of one or more phenomena of the universe, either natural or human. All the hexagrams put together were supposed to represent symbolically all that had happened in the universe, in heaven, in earth, in the complexity of human affairs. The *I Ching* is indeed one of the most remarkable treatises in the history of philosophy. Its significance is due to the fact that it uses the simple symbols to represent the complexity of nature, and abstract ideas to symbolize concrete objects. In this respect, this is not merely a book of philosophy, but a work of art as well—a combination of the abstract and concrete, with the aesthetic symbols revealing depth of knowledge.

There has been a great controversy as to how much Confucius contributed to the *I Ching*. The traditional view maintains that the Sage arranged the book and wrote the appendices and commentaries. The heretics, on the other hand, deny his authorship altogether, considering all the extraneous material as forgeries by later writers. And finally, modern scholars particularly trained in textual criticism maintain that, even if in his later years Confucius was extremely fascinated by the *I Ching*, these appendices could never have been written by the Sage.

Not one of these theories has been conclusively established, and this is not the place to undertake an extended analysis of the controversy. Probably the most plausible assumption is that these appendices must have been the product not of one but of many authors, who gave the *I* various interpretations and read into it their own ideas, but they were not composed until the latter part of the Chou dynasty. This theory explains why its simple symbols can be freely applied in various ways; thus both Confucians and Taoists all used the *I Ching* to express their ideas, and so the *I Ching* serves as a bridge between the teachings of the opposing schools. Let us turn, for illustration, to Chapter II of the *Shuo Kua*, the "Discourses on the Trigrams" (the eighth appendix):

> In ancient times when the Sages made the *I*, their purpose was to follow the principles of the natures [things possess] and of the different lots [which Heaven decrees]. Therefore they established the *Tao* of Heaven designated as the *Yin* and the *Yang*. They determined the *Tao* of Earth designated as the yielding and the firm. They determined the *Tao* of Man designated as *jen* (human-heartedness) and *yi* (righteousness). They combined these three Powers and doubled them; hence in the *I* each *kua* (hexagram) was formed by six lines.

In this passage we can see that the Confucian principles of *jen* and *yi* are brought into harmony with the Taoist concept of Heaven-and-Earth. This conception, in fact, may be traced back to the Sinitic belief in the interrelationship of man and natural environment: Heaven, Earth, and Man are inseparable, and they must be kept in harmony.

Li Ching or Books of Rituals and Etiquette

The fourth classic, the *Li Ching,* is actually a collection of texts dealing with rituals and etiquette, which governed the moral, social, and religious activities of the Chou aristocrats. These texts were originally religious, and used only in sacrifices, but later became ethicised as social and political institutions. Thus the observance of *li* (rites) was the ethical prod of the feudal system, and the *li* permeated life in all its aspects. It might be defined as the mode of living of the nobility in ancient China, and this mode of living included religion, politics, and ethics, the last being the most important.

Long before Confucius' time, there existed an unwritten code of rituals and etiquette, known as *li,* but during the Chou period, it was defined, fixed, and set down in writing. There must have been many discrepancies between the written *li* and those of the past ages—just as there must have been differences among traditional *li* of the various feudal states, some of which, as a result of ignorance, devoted themselves to practices contrary to the true spirit of *li.*

Confucius, as a teacher, studied the *li* and stressed its origin and significance. He criticized the debased practices of the time, terming *li* without sentiment as nothing more than mock ceremony. Moreover, Confucius popularized the code of *li* and insisted that not only the nobles but the common people as well should be governed by the *li.*

The *Li Ching* was the most imperfectly preserved of the Five Confucian Classics. The feudal lords, in their eagerness to seize imperial power, variously mutilated *li* records which laid any restraint on their improper conduct. These *li* records were further damaged after the "Ch'in fire" in 213 B.C. The three prominent treatises on the subject of *li,* which we have today, were the works of a later period, though they all may stem from the Confucian tradition. The three *li* books, often called the *Three Rituals,* and also known as the *Li Ching,* are the *I Li* (the *Book of Etiquette and Ceremonial*), the *Chou Li* (the *Book of Chou Rituals*), and the *Li Chi* (the *Book of Rites*).

The *I Li*—seventeen chapters in its present form—consists of a series of minute and systematic directions for the feudal aristocrats on such ceremonial occasions as capping, marriage, mourning, archery contests, reception of guests, and ceremonial drinking. These chapters contain no dialogue or anecdotes, being simple descriptions, devoid of literary embellishment. This book gives us vivid pictures of many phases of the life of ancient times. It was probably written after the time of Confucius.

The *Chou Li*, also known as the *Chou Kuan*, is an elaborate description of the bureaucratic system and governmental structure of Chou times. The work is composed of six sections, each dealing with a major component of the Chou government: (1) *T'ien Kuan* or Institute of Heaven—the Prime Ministry; (2) *Ti Kuan* or Institute of Earth—the Department of Education and Social Welfare; (3) *Ch'un Kuan* or Institute of Spring—the Department of Ceremonies and Protocol; (4) *Hsia Kuan* or Institute of Summer—Department of Defense and Security; (5) *Ch'iu Kuan* or Institute of Autumn—the Department of Justice and Punishment; (6) *Tung Kuan* or Institute of Winter—Department of Public Works and Economic Production. In its present form the last section (lost) is supplied by a document called *K'ao Kung Chi* or the *Record of the Inspection of Works*. It was generally agreed that the work was the product of the fourth or fifth century B.C., perhaps with alterations and interpolations by Han scholars. In spite of its dubious historicity, this work, with its detailed descriptions of the functions of the various departments of the dynastic government, is the most important Confucian literature regarding administration and government. Moreover, the six institutes remained the equivalent of cabinet departments of state until the end of the nineteenth century.

The most famous of the *Li* books is the *Li Chi*, which consists of "the records composed by the pupils of the seventy

(Confucian) disciples," representing an encyclopedia of Confucian teachings of late Chou, Ch'in, and Han times. These *li* records were in the first century B.C. compiled and edited by *li* experts, particularly two members of the Tai family, Tai Te (the Elder Tai), and Tai Sheng (the Younger Tai). The *li* collection of the Younger Tai consists of forty-six records, with commentaries by Cheng Hsüan (A.D. 127–200) and known as the *Li Chi*, or *Hsiao-Tai Li Chi*. The *li* collection of the Elder Tai consists of thirty-nine records, with commentaries by Lu Pien of the Northern Chou period (A.D. 557–580) and known as the *Ta-Tai Li Chi*. The latter work originally consisted of eighty-four records, but forty-six have been lost. It was not until near the close of the second century A.D. that the titles of the two *li* collections were established. The *Li Chi* was constructed not by the writing of original articles on the subject treated but by compiling and arranging various texts of different periods written by different authors. Hence the forty-nine chapters in its present form are dissimilar not merely in length and in content but in their origins and style. The last two of the Four Books, the *Ta Hsüeh* and the *Chung Yung*, were taken by the Neo-Confucian scholars from the *Li Chi*. On these two books the Neo-Confucians hoped to erect their complete philosophical system.

Ch'un Ch'iu or *Spring and Autumn Annals*

Another group of writings comprised the historical records of the various states, known as the *Ch'un Ch'iu* or the *Spring and Autumn Annals*. *Ch'un Ch'iu* owes its name to the tradition of prefixing each entry with the year, month, day and season when the event took place. Since spring then included summer, and autumn included winter, entries are all preceded by one of these two terms. The *Ch'un Ch'iu* of the various states existed before Confucius, and the Sage, according to tradition, compiled the *Annals* from the records he found in the archives of Lu. The *Annals* is simply brief chronological records of the major events as they happened in the State of Lu from 722 B.C. to 481 B.C. While this is a good way to collect materials, it is hardly sufficient to produce what would be classified as history. However, an elaborate system of interpretation has been worked out purporting to reveal the philosophical significance of the words and phrases describing persons or events recorded in the *Ch'un Ch'iu*.

The *Ch'un Ch'iu* would have been lost had it not been for the three major commentaries written on it, all supposed to have been handed down from the latter part of the fifth century B.C. Since the Han dynasty these commentaries—*Tso Chüan* or *Tso Commentary*, the *Kung-yang* and the *Ku-liang* commentaries—have themselves been venerated as classics. The *Kung-yang* and *Ku-liang* commentaries, explaining the why and the wherefore of the diction and word order of the entries in the *Annals*, contain too little narrative to be considered as historical or literary work. The *Tso Commentary*, in contrast, has been praised very highly as literature. The book utilizes the chronicles of the various states during the period, expanding the narration, and so looks like a news story as compared with the headline. The narratives contain a large admixture of legend and romance and are noted for meticulous description and vivid phraseology.

These five categories of ancient writings we have mentioned make up the *Wu Ching* or the Five Classics. The Sixth Classic on Music, though often mentioned in early writing, is lost. It is only in the works of Hsün Tzu that we can understand the part played by music as a ritual experience and a communal entertainment in ancient times. Hsün Tzu in Chapter 20 of his work also gave a good description of the various instruments used in ancient China. Chapters XIX and XLV of the *Li Chi*, dealing with music and drinking festivity, were taken from this chapter in the *Hsün Tzu*.

CHAPTER 1

Pre-Confucian Philosophical and Religious Thought

Animism

Chinese religious thinking grew out of animism. In addition to the worship of ancestors, there was reverence for the deities of the sun, moon, stars, wind, rain, and sacred mountains and rivers, whose blessings were regarded as necessary to the well-being of man. However, forces and objects of nature were not the only deities which the early Chinese venerated, and to which they offered sacrifices. Among other divine beings worshipped there were deities of the earth and grain—a sort of agricultural deities, who, they believed, exerted a very definite influence on human affairs. The deity of the earth was symbolized by the *she*, the so-called 'altar of the land'; it was also known as the *hou tu* or 'Queen Earth,' somewhat like our 'Mother Earth.' The *she* had a good deal of control over the fertility of the soil. The deity of grain was symbolized by the *chi*, a kind of plant, also known as *hou chi*, to which sacrifices were offered for an abundant harvest. These agricultural deities were frequently mentioned together as *she chi*, 'land and grain,' or 'the altar of land and grain.' But *she chi* was also recognized as a religious and symbolic center of the state, where certain elaborate ceremonies, especially those in connection with military expeditions, were held. All these religious beliefs prevailed before the era of the Chou dynasty.

In ancient documents and on oracle bones, we find frequent references to a supreme deity called *Ti* or *Shang Ti* (the Lord-on-High),[1] whose sway extended over all deities and creations. The position of *Ti* in heaven was somewhat like that of the king on the earth. The Supreme Deity had control over rain, and dominated man and his activities by either sending down rain to the earth or holding back, thus creating droughts and famine. On the oracle bones we read: "Will *Ti* decree famine for the year?" "No more rain and *Ti* will starve us!"[2] *Ti* was also much concerned with the making of war, and brought victory to the army. For instance, on one oracle bone we find a prayer for victory to *Ti* about the king's military expedition against the tribe *Kung-feng*.[3] *Ti* also had the power to send down good luck or misfortune to the world according to his pleasure. All these divine powers, and others, he wielded over human lives.

The blessing and protection of the Supreme Deity, essential to the welfare of men and most significantly that of the ruling house, were to be secured by the proper performance of ritual and sacrifice in honor of him. The ceremonies for *Ti* were conducted by the king in the suburbs of the capital. Just how this Supreme Deity was originally conceived by the early Chinese, we cannot tell. In view of the close relationship between *Ti* and the ruling house, the possibility is that *Shang Ti* was the chief deity or even a deified ancestor of the ruling house. It was a basic belief of great antiquity that the spirits of ancestors lived in heaven, sitting near *Ti*, for they were often spoken of in the oracle bones as descending, sending down blessings, and so forth. One oracle bone reads: "Hsia I pays homage to *Ti*,"[4] Hsia I being an ancestor of the ruling house, also known as Tsu I (ruled 1525–1510 B.C.). Since it was up to *Ti* to send rain sufficient for the year, the ancestors might use their influence to prevail upon *Ti* not to send down rain as a measure of punishment against wicked kings. Among the

Shang kings, wu Ting (reigned 1324–1266 B.C.) took a great
interest in his ancestors and in religious ritual, sacrificing a
great deal to his most distant ancestors. In the oracle bones wu
Ting was found to ask on several occasions such questions as:
"Is it true that Wang-hai prevents rain?" "Is it true that Shang-
chia prevents rain?"[5] Both Wang-hai and Shang-chia were
Shang ancestors of quite remote generations. However, it was
customary for later kings to sacrifice to more immediate ancestors.

Thus the early Chinese basically believed in *Ti* or *Shang Ti*
(a supreme deity who presided over heaven much as the king
governed the world) and in a variety of heavenly and earthly
deities, who exercised influence over human affairs. However,
it was still the ancestor cult that played the most significant
role in the religious life of the early Chinese. In this connection,
the following statement from Tung Tso-pin's "An Interpretation of the Ancient Chinese Civilization" is worth quoting:

> The one hundred thousand pieces of oracle bones and shells
> contain little but the questions the reverential Yin (Shang)
> kings put to their ancestors and the answers in the forms of
> cracks which the bones and shells produced when they were
> scorched.[6]

On the basis of the oracle bones, it was evident that the
principal possession of the reigning king was his ancestors.
There is good reason for this. They not only gave him legitimate title to rule, but had a good deal of power to intercede
with the Supreme Deity in Heaven to send down blessings or
calamities. The religious ceremonies for ancestors were elaborate, with offerings of food, occasionally of human life. Under
the Chou the practice of human sacrifice gradually disappeared.

The cult of ancestor-worship was by no means limited to
the kings in the early period. In the oracle bones we find little
information about any but the ruling house, but the common
people also worshipped their forebears. Ancestor worship was
the most fundamental and widespread Chinese religious belief

and practice, interwoven into the very fabric of life. The main ritual activities of the state centered around the ancestral temple of the ruling house. According to the ancient records, the Chou kings, like the Shang kings whom they succeeded, had lavishly sacrificed to their ancestors and believed that the latter's blessings and protection in various undertakings were of utmost importance. Even at the beginning of the Chou period we find it recorded that the ceremonial rules and rites of ancestor worship were not only religious, but also legal obligations; to neglect them, or to perform them improperly, would bring about condemnation and calamity.

Like *she chi,* or "the altar of land and grain," the king's ancestral temple was also recognized as the center of national affairs, where important activities of the state (such as military planning and state banquets) took place. The importance of the ancestral temple and the *she chi,* twin centers of spiritual forces assuring prosperity in peace and victory in war, is shown by the fact that when a state was conquered it was customary to destroy the two cult centers. Only in this way could the ancestral spirits and local deities favoring the former regime be counteracted.

Basic to the religious tradition of the Shang period was a belief in an intimate and mutual relationship between the dead and the living, the other world and this world, as well as between various deities and spirits and human beings. The spiritual beings shared a reciprocal dependence with men, bestowing blessings in return for sacrifices. The relationship of mutual dependence, with its expectation of blessings in exchange for sacrifices, has been a popular belief of the Chinese. It persists to this day.

The ancient Chinese thought the other world peopled with both departed ancestors and a diverse pantheon of local deities. These deities, most of whom descended from men,[7] became so entangled in human affairs that they had a great affinity with humanity. Man and the divine were inextricably intertwined and completely involved with each other. They were inseparable, and they must be kept in harmony. This belief points to the humanistic temperament of the Chinese people in the matter of religion.

The Rise of Humanism

The religious beliefs of the Shang people were gradually transformed during the Chou period. As popularly practiced at that time, these beliefs combined sophisticated ideas and gross superstition, but in simplifying and modifying them, the Chou gave them all humanistic interpretations. Though they did not deny the existence and power of nature deities and ancestral spirits, yet they seemed to adopt the skeptical attitude as expressed in the *Li Chi* (the *Book of Rites*):

> The Yin (Shang) honor spiritual beings, serve them, and put them ahead of ceremonies. . . . The Chou honor ceremonies and highly value the bestowing (of favors). Then they serve spiritual beings and respect them, but keep them at a distance.[8]

In the Chou literature and bronze inscriptions we find an important concept of *T'ien* (Heaven) used interchangeably with *Shang Ti* (the Supreme Deity). For instance, in the *Shih Ching* (the *Book of Poetry*)[9] one poem says:

> *T'ien* decreed the Black Bird to descend
> And give birth to [the ancestor of] Shang:
> He abode in the vast land of Yin.
> Of old, *Ti* charged the martial T'ang[10]
> To set up boundaries of the four quarters.

(Ode 303)

Similarly in the *Shu Ching* (the *Book of History*):[11] "The King said: 'Come, people, and hear to my words. Not would I like to bring about this irregular proceeding, but the sovereign of Hsia has committed many crimes and *T'ien* has decreed his extermination. . . . I fear *Shang Ti* and dare not but punish him' " (Bk III, Sec. 1). Clearly in the Chou period both *Shang Ti* and *T'ien* were interchangeably used as names for the same deity. Originally they were probably distinct, *Shang Ti*, as the supreme deity over an elaborate hierarchy of spirits, being more nearly an anthropomorphic and personal conception, and the depersonalized *T'ien* representing a cosmic moral order and divine power, being concerned with the actions of man and as a source of "mandate" for the legitimacy of the ruling dynasty. Thus the *Shu Ching* says: "*T'ien*, having produced people below, appointed for them rulers and teachers" (Bk I, Sec. 4). It was in this light that the Chou kings were commonly called *T'ien Tzu* (the Son of Heaven). This was the religious belief of the Chou, which thus involved ethical and political considerations.

In this connection, there was an important concept called *T'ien-ming* (the Mandate of Heaven) which buttressed the political creed of the Chou. Heaven was conceived as a great deity of humanity and did not come into direct contact with the people but appointed as his medium on earth a line of kings to rule under his mandate. Heaven, if displeased with the wickedness of a reigning house, could transfer his mandate to another house to form a new and more virtuous dynasty. The Chou rulers claimed his mandate and thus justified their conquest of the Shang and their domination of the country.

The following passage from the *Shu Ching* offers a good illustration of this concept.

> Duke Chou[12] said: "Prince Shih,[13] Heaven, without pity, sent ruin to Yin (Shang). Yin having lost the Mandate (of Heaven), we of the Chou have received it instead. But I dare not say with certainty that our heritage will forever remain with fortune. Even though Heaven should bless and protect us, yet I'd not dare to say with certainty our end would not result in misfortune.
>
> "Oh! your Highness has yourself said: 'It depends on ourselves!' So dare I not rest on the Mandate of *Shang Ti* and thus fail to think of the awe-inspiring majesty of Heaven; nor dare

I suppose that our people would never complain and rebel. It is [a matter which depends mainly] on men [like you]! If our descendants prove utterly unable to reverence [Heaven] above and [the people] below, and so bring to an end the glory of their forefathers, could you, remaining at home, be unaware of it?

"The Mandate of Heaven is not easy [to preserve], and so is Heaven hard [to rely on]. [Those rulers] lost the mandate because of their inability to emulate and carry on the reverence and the brilliant virtue of their forefathers. At the present time, so insignificant I am that I am incapable of rectifying [our king]; I would rather cultivate the glory of our forefathers and extend it to our young king."

Duke Chou also said: "Heaven is not to be trusted. My way is simply to extend the virtue of our peace-establishing king, so that Heaven will have no occasion to revoke his mandate received by King Wen [the founder of the Chou dynasty who ruled 1171–22 B.C.] . . ." (Bk V, Sec. 5).

Obvious in the passage quoted above is a basic belief in the divine sanction of the political order and the grave responsibility of the ruler to fulfill his moral duties to Heaven and to the people. The king ruled with the Mandate of Heaven because of his own virtue and the glory of his ancestors. In other words, he received the mandate in trust, subject to revocation if he proved unable to set a good example and to glorify his ancestors. The way in which the king might set up a moral leadership so as not to lose the Mandate of Heaven became a major concern of the Chou statesmen and one of the key problems of Chinese thought.

In spite of what has been said, the Chou were not agnostics, denying the existence and power of intervention of Heaven. But virtue, they insisted, was far more important than sacrifices in obtaining the blessings and protection of Heaven. They assumed that Heaven would throw its weight on the side of virtuous conduct of men. In this manner the concept of Heaven was conceived to be an impersonal ethical force, a cosmic counterpart of the moral responsibility in man, a guarantee that virtue would be rewarded and vice punished. This was a far cry from Heaven conceived as a supreme deity controlling the destiny of man or the future of a dynasty and rewarding or punishing as He pleased. With this change in religious faith, it was only to be expected that the Chinese of the Chou would place the emphasis on moral code and not on purely ritual practices.

It was in this light that religious ceremonies underwent an enormous change. The elaborate ceremonies, which were of many kinds and grades, contained much of superstition and mythology. During the Chou period, humanistic interpretations of these ceremonies and especially those of sacrifices led to a search for ethical ideas in the purely ceremonial practices. These we find in the Chou literature and especially its later philosophical writings such as the *Tso Chuan* or *Tso's Commentary* on the *Spring and Autumn Annals*,[14] the *Kuo Yü* or the *Discourses of the States*,[15] *Li Chi* or the *Book of Rites*, and the *Hsün Tzu*.[16]

For instance, the *Kuo Yü* says:

> Sacrifice is designed to show one filial piety, and give peace to the people, as well as to pacify the country and make the people settled. . . . to make illustrious their sacrifice to the early ancestors, (the people) are reverent and solemn as if (the spirits) were observing them. Thereby local friends and relatives through marriage, elder and younger brothers and blood relatives are united. Thereby all sorts of abuses are stopped; the evils of slander are eliminated; those who are friends are united; relatives are drawn into a common bond; and both superiors and inferiors are put at rest, so as to extend and strengthen the family. . . . It is through these sacrifices that the unity of the people is strengthened (*Ch'u Yü*, II, 8).

The function of sacrifice, we see, is to bring all the local clan members and relatives together into one place, and at the same time to cultivate not only unity but also a proper sentiment of respect and reverence among men. With this humanistic interpretation, ceremonies, especially sacrifices, became a means of "strengthening the unity of the people," rather than a purely ritual practice to "serve the spirits." It was a means of strengthening society through religious ritual. Likewise during the Chou period we find in the cult of ancestor-worship an increased emphasis on its ethical function of integrating the family group and cultivating kinship values such as filial piety, family loyalty, and continuity of the family lineage.

During the Chou period Chinese philosophical and religious thought was dominated by this humanistic ideal. Its greatest contribution to Chinese thought lies in its rationalizing religious beliefs and transforming purely ritual practices into a universal system of ethics. Before the end of the Chou period the various schools of thought developed within the stream of what may be called humanism—not a humanism that denied the existence and power of natural forces and objects, but one that placed emphasis on the interrelationship of man and nature. This is what is known as the theory of "the unity of Heaven and man" as enunciated by Chinese philosophers. How humanism came about and developed can best be illustrated in the study of Confucianism.

CHAPTER 2

The Rise of Confucianism: Confucius

His Life

Of all the great philosophers of China, Confucius is best known to the world. The name Confucius is a Latinized Western form of the Chinese K'ung Fu Tzu, which literally means Master K'ung. His family name was K'ung, and his given name was Ch'iu. Later he was called Chung-ni (Ni the Younger), for his crippled brother was called Po-ni (Ni the Elder). His birth date is obscure, but that traditionally given, 551 B.C., cannot be far wrong. He was born in Lu (modern Ch'u Fu in Shantung), the center of Chou culture. K'ung's family traced its ancestry to the ducal house of Sung (in central Honan), which was descended from the royal house of Shang, the dynasty that preceded the Chou. His ancestors had thus all been men of eminence in politics and letters. Because of political troubles, his great grandfather had lost his noble position and moved to Lu. His father, the elder K'ung Shu-liang Ho (624–549? B.C.) was a distinguished soldier who died when Confucius was only three years old.

Not much is known of the Sage's childhood under the care and instruction of his widowed mother. Probably his first schooling began at the age of seven. We learn from the *Lun Yü* (the *Analects* II, 4) that at fifteen he had set his mind on learning, but most probably he was largely self-taught. Because of his father's death, K'ung's family was in straitened circumstances, and the young Confucius was at first unable to follow the path of pure scholarship. He began his career as a granary overseer in his district and had a successful term of office. The following year he was placed in charge of grazing grounds, and under his management the cattle and sheep were properly fattened. At a later period the Sage told his disciples: "When I was young I was in humble circumstances; for this reason I acquired some skills in a number of lowly pursuits" (IX–6).

At nineteen, Confucius was married and a son was born a year later. At the birth of the son, the reigning duke of Lu sent a pair of carp, the traditional symbol of domestic felicity and fertility. To commemorate the gift, the infant was given the name Li (carp), and later was called Po-yü (Fish the Elder). Nothing is known of other children except that Confucius had at least one daughter, who was married to one of his disciples.

In 528 B.C., Confucius abandoned his public service to mourn the death of his mother. During the three years' mourning, he refrained from sensual indulgence and activities and devoted himself to the study of ancient *li* (rites) and institutions. We do not know what position he took after the period of mourning was over. Probably he commenced his career as a public teacher, gathering to his door a group of aspiring young men to be instructed in the useful knowledge of *li* and its accompanying arts. By the age of thirty, he already commanded public attention and the respect of the great for the mastery of *li*. For instance, in 518 B.C., while lying on his deathbed, Meng Hsi-tzu, head of one of the three leading families in Lu, told his two sons to study under Confucius. It was through the influence of the two young scions of the Meng family that Confucius was later sent by Duke Chao of Lu to visit Lo, the imperial capital of Chou, to observe the relics of lost imperial greatness.

Although Confucius did not remain at Lo for long, the visit gave him a deeper understanding of the cultural inheritance and opened up new vistas for his further pursuit, while at the same time convincing him of the greatness of Chou culture. Upon returning to Lu, Confucius continued his work of teaching. His fame greatly increased, and all sorts of young men, eager to be instructed in the knowledge of *li* and the art of government, continued to flock to him, contributing more and more to his reputation as a great teacher and a great master of ceremonials.

Not until he was past fifty did Confucius enter government service. At the age of fifty-two (500 B.C.), he was made the chief magistrate of Cheng-tu, an outlying town west of the Lu capital, and was soon promoted to the position of Minister of Justice, next in rank only to the ministries of instruction, works and war, held by the chiefs of the three powerful clans. Not only did the new minister effect immediate improvement in the manners and morals of the people, but he also strengthened the ducal house and weakened the influence of the ministers. However, just at the very moment when Confucius had put his own state on the right track, evil forces gathered to wreak vengeance on him. As a result of political intrigue arising from the jealousy and fears of neighbors of Lu, he had to hand in his resignation and leave Lu with a handful of students. This was in the year 497 B.C. For the next fourteen years (497–484 B.C.), Confucius wandered vainly from state to state in search of patronage and opportunities for working out his ideal of government. When at last he was recalled to Lu by a new duke, he was already an old man of sixty-eight, hardly able to resume his political career. Since his direct attempts had often been thwarted by official jealousy, he henceforth endeavored to attain his ends by less direct but more certain means. He devoted himself more than ever to the instruction of youth and to the editing and recording of ancient documents, which were later recognized as classics to be studied by students in both private and public schools.

In 482 B.C., Confucius lost his only son; in 481 B.C., his favorite student, Yen Hui (also known as Yen Yuen); and in 479 B.C., he himself died at the age of seventy-three. He was buried near his native town, in the district of Ch'u Fu, where his tomb temple is still to be seen.

The career of the Sage was centered on three important goals: to serve government, to teach youth, and to transmit the ancient culture to posterity. These three lines of activity were more or less overlapping. In so far as we know, Confucius' great ambition lay in politics but there he met with varied and uncertain success. He had on several occasions been called upon to advise reigning dukes and ministers on state affairs. He was also engaged in administration that had helped to acquaint him with the actual workings of government. All these experiences contributed much to the Confucian philosophy, which has exerted the greatest influence on Chinese government for the last twenty-five centuries.

However, the greatest achievement of Confucius was in education. He was a teacher of great skill and reputation, with a group of aspiring young disciples of all descriptions, from the lowest as well as the highest social strata, at his side. Bearing as little as "a bundle of meat" for tuition, they came to be instructed in various branches of knowledge based upon the "Six Arts," more commonly known as the "Six Classics." These are the *I* (Changes), the *Shih* (Poetry), the *Shu* (History), the *Li* (Rituals), the *Yüeh* (Music), and the *Ch'un Ch'iu* (*Spring and Autumn Annals*), which had existed before the time of Confucius and constituted the cultural legacy of the past. This form of education was the great innovation of the Chou period. Prior to the time of Confucius, all branches of learning had been in the official custody of hereditary aristocrats. Confucius was the first to offer to instruct the private individual and to set up a sort of school for all young men, irrespective of their status and means. Confucius was thus the first teacher in Chinese history to make education available to the common people. He believed that "in education, there should be no class distinction" (XV–38).

Our discussion of Confucius' career would be incomplete without a word on his contribution to the ancient classics. Opinion is divided as to the originality of this contribution. We shall not go into this controversy here, because it is clearly a matter for textual criticism. In this perspective, it is extremely important to recognize that Confucius was, as he himself said, "a transmitter and not a creator, a believer in and lover of antiquity" (VII-1). As a lover of antiquity he removed the ancient documents from official custody, arranged them in order, and put them into the form of what were later known as the Six Classics. These were the source books of the Confucian school. From them Confucius gathered his fund of wisdom. Upon them he built his ethical and political philosophy. With them he transmitted the cultural heritage of the past. The significance of Confucius as a transmitter lies in his attempt to provide a justification for ancient institutions and principles underlying the ancient classics. In this way Confucius was more than a mere transmitter, for in transmitting he had made some important innovations and added some principles which are highly original and creative. This tradition of creating while transmitting, as handed down by the followers of Confucius such as Mencius and Hsün Tzu, enabled the Confucian school to forge ethics with politics, the past and the present, into a unified system. This creative evolution is characteristic of the Confucian philosophy.

Generally speaking, the thought of Confucius is found in the Six Classics, but is known through the *Lun Yü* or the *Analects*, a collection of scattered sayings by Confucius and some of his disciples, recorded by the disciples of the Confucian school. For this reason, the *Lun Yü* furnishes important source materials for the study of the thought of Confucius. In the *Lun Yü* we see the image of Confucius as well as his teachings, as in the New Testament we see the figure of Christ.

His Thought

As background for our study of his thought, let us first consider the views of Confucius on religion. Like the Shang, the Chou believed in the existence and power of intervention of supernatural beings. As noted above, this religious belief, under the influence of humanism, had been gradually revised during the Chou period. In the time of Confucius, Heaven was seldom conceived of as an anthropomorphic being, and stood more frequently for a vaguely conceived moral force in the universe. Even more important, sacrifice was considered rather a barter transaction than a purely ritual practice. Though basically moralistic and not theological, Confucius' ethics was strongly tinged by religious conviction, but he rationalized religion by new interpretations and read into it new ideas.

In the *Lun Yü* (XI–11), we read:

> Chi Lu (Tzu Lu, one of his disciples) asked how one should serve spirits, and the Master said: "You are not yet able to serve men, how can you serve spirits?"
>
> Then the disciples asked about death, and the Master said: "You do not yet understand life; how can you understand death?"

From these and certain other passages, it is clear that Confucius attached great importance to humanity, stressing man's life in this world, not his eternal life in the other world. This explains why Confucius was not, as sometimes supposed, a religious prophet and why his teachings, unlike Christianity, Buddhism, and Mohammedanism, remain to this day a philosophy and a system of ethics.

In the *Lun Yü*, there is another statement made by Confucius about spirits:

> Fan Ch'ih [a disciple] asked about wisdom, and the Master said: "Devote yourself to these duties which are proper to the people; and respect the spirits but maintain the proper distance from them. This may be called wisdom" (VI–22).

Confucius' principal concern was man and the "duties which are proper to the people"; he studiously shunned all questions that enter into ontological subtleties or concern the supernatural. His thought is more in the nature of an ethical system than a religion and as such it is essentially of this world in outlook and rationalistic in approach. All his teachings are imbued with this central human concern.

Let us turn now to the life ideal of Confucius. In an interesting conversation with his disciples Yen Hui and Tzu Lu, Confucius gave a good illustration of his life ideal:

> Once Yen Yuan [Yen Hui] and Chi Lu [Tzu Lu] were with him, and the Master said: "Why don't you each tell me your wish?"
>
> "I should like," said Tzu Lu, "to have carriages and horses, and to be clad in furs, so that I can share them with my friends. Even if they were worn out, I would not mind."
>
> "I should like," said Yen Yuan, "to make no boast of my abilities, or display my good deeds."
>
> Then Tzu Lu [turned to the Master and] said: "We should like, Sir, to hear of your wish."
>
> "I should like," said the Master, "to bring security to the aged, to be loyal to my friends, and to be affectionate with the young " (V–25).

These ideals of Confucius and his two disciples are the same in that they express proper regard for other men, but they differ in their approaches and attitudes. Tzu Lu was utilitarian: he wanted to share "his carriages, horses, and fur coats" with his friends, to boast of his generosity. Yen Hui was moral: he felt morally obliged to devote his "abilities and good deeds" to the service of others. This moral obligation, as conceived here, is a "categorical imperative" leading to unselfconscious efforts for the good of others. Any action which is done in this way is a righteous action. Confucius went further: he wanted "to nourish the aged and to cherish the young," not because of the moral obligation but because of a sense of fellow-feeling with other men. In this light, what he did as a benefit to others is not only a righteous action, but is also a *jen* (human-hearted) action.[1] Hence Confucius has been often known as a man of *jen*.

It is obvious that the ideas of Confucius which express his life ideal are not abstract ideas, but instead are visions of a cultivated mind, imbued with a profound sense of purpose and an intense concern for the well-being of his fellow men. These ideas were reflected in his own life and are embodied in the concept of *jen*. In the *Lun Yü*, we find that *jen* has a great scope and a great depth, yet it is familiar and appears to be simple and practical; it has flexibility and versatility, yet it dominates the thought of Confucius as the central thesis of the whole system. His ethics, his politics, his life ideal—all flow from this governing doctrine.

The ideograph for *jen* is composed of two characters, "man" and "two," showing stress on the relationship between man and his fellow men. Confucius maintained that human relations should be based on the moral element *jen* in the individual, the natural compassion of human heart. In the *Lun Yü*, we read:

> Fan Chi [a disciple] asked about *jen*, and the Master said: "To love men" (XII–22).

Love is an emotion common to mankind, but love that arises from *jen* manifests itself in different degrees of intensity. It originates with the bonds of a common parentage and extends to other relationships until it culminates in the stage of *jen*. To be more specific, the basis of *jen* is to be found in the virtues of filial piety (*hsiao*) and fraternal love (*ti*) (I–2).

> "A youth should be filial at home, and fraternal when abroad. He should be earnest and sincere; he should show an affection for all and be disposed towards *jen*" (I–6).

The concepts of filial piety and fraternal love express the same unselfish human feeling—filial piety signifying a state of spiritual communion in the eternity of time, and fraternal love signifying a state of communion in the infinity of space. Confucius, with his keen sense of practicality, made the virtues of filial piety and fraternal love the cornerstones of the social structure. By extending them in time and in space, and diffusing their influence through all other related virtues, he made them both the bond of social solidarity and the connection between succeeding generations. In their broader extension, filial piety and fraternal love become the rational basis for the love due to men. They become *jen*.

In the *Lun Yü*, two other similar concepts are introduced: *chung* (conscientiousness), being faithful to one's self; and *shu* (altruism), having proper regard for one's fellow men. The former is the state of mind when one is completely honest with one's self; the latter is the state of mind when one is in complete understanding and sympathy with other men. The Chinese character for *chung* is made of two components: "middle" and "heart." With one's heart in the very center, one will be faithful to one's self. And one will do one's very best for others. In Confucius' words:

> A man of *jen*, desiring to be established himself, seeks to establish others; desiring himself to succeed, he helps others to succeed (VI–28).

Chung is the positive way to practice *jen*.

The Chinese word *shu* has the meaning of "as one's heart," that is, to do unto others as your heart prompts you. It is indeed a sense of fellow-feeling with other men—to extend one's self to include others. As to the significance of *shu*, Confucius said: "Do not do to others what you do not want done to yourself" (XV–24). This is the negative way to practice *jen*.

The concepts of *chung* and *shu* are the same as those of *hsiao* and *ti*. The latter refer principally to the relations within the family, while the former have a wider, less specific import. In both cases, the concern is for a state of mind where true and unselfish love reigns and one extends and develops one's own goodness to include one's fellow men. This is the starting point of the practice of *jen*. Therefore Confucius said: "To be able from one's self to draw a parallel in dealing with others is the direction of *jen*" (VI–28).

In the strict sense of the word, *jen* is the virtue of being faithful to one's self and having a sense of fellow-feeling with one's fellow men. However, we must remember that *jen* is a natural feeling that comes directly and spontaneously from the human heart. Men with this natural feeling recognize that they must live in a community of mutual friendship and joyful harmony. Confucius contended that faith in such an idealistic state of affairs becoming a reality was based on the cultivation and perfection of goodness not only in one's self, but everyone else.

Confucius' doctrine of *jen*, essentially a man-to-man relationship, is a moral system which is both practical and practicable. Without any trace of the metaphysical and the supernatural, it is readily understood; its teachings, replete with wisdom and common sense, can be applied in all human relations. Therefore, not only is *jen* a supreme moral principle in human relations, but it is also a practical morality easy to attain. Confucius said:

> Is *jen* so far away? I want to have *jen*, and lo! *jen* is at hand (VII–29).
> Is anyone able even for a single day to apply his energy to the practice of *jen*? I have never seen anyone who lacked the necessary energy (IV–6).

Everyone is able to take his own feelings as guide in dealing with others. So simple is the practice of *jen*, yet one does not always do what one ought to do, because one is much concerned with profit. This is why "the Master seldom spoke of profit; his attachment was to Fate [*Ming*]² and *jen*" (XI–1).

Confucius' life ideal was a vision of how *jen* is realized at large. It consists of doing one's very best for the sake of others. For Confucius, it is not sufficient to cultivate good in one's self, it is important to extend one's goodness to include others. For Confucius it is not sufficient to do what one ought to do, it is more important to disregard what is external to this moral obligation. Confucius offered in himself a good example of a life dominated by the doctrine of *jen*. He traveled through many states in his time seeking opportunity to test this doctrine in actual practice. Although his efforts were in vain, he was not disappointed. He was much ridiculed by contemporary recluses and Taoists,[3] who spurned as futile all his efforts at reform. In the *Lun Yü* we read:

> When Tzu Lu arrived to pass the night in the city of Shi-men, the gatekeeper asked: "Where are you coming from?" "From Confucius."
> "Is he not the man who is undertaking something even though he knows what he does is in vain?" (XIV–41).

The last sentence shows what some thought of Confucius.

As to himself, Confucius said: "If my *tao* (a way of life)[4] is to prevail, it is Fate. If my *tao* is to be rejected, it is also Fate" (XIV–38). While Confucius made the best effort to realize the ideal of his *tao*, at the same time he insisted that Fate would determine whether this ideal succeeded or failed. In other words, Confucius did his best for the sake of others, but he left his success or failure to Fate. As already noted, the word *Fate* may be interpreted either as "the Decree of Heaven," or as "the existent conditions of the universe." Whatever is meant by the word, Fate is something inevitable, independent of effort. It has to do with forces beyond man's control. Hence the best way of life, according to Confucius, is to do one's best, without regard for success or failure. To act in this way, as Confucius said, is "to know Fate."

"To know Fate means to acknowledge the inevitability of the world as it exists and so to disregard one's success or failure."[5] Still Confucius was not a fatalist, nor did he intend to rely on Fate. On the contrary, he repeatedly insisted on the importance of individual effort and the moral obligation to do one's best for the sake of others. Here is the key, then, to Confucius' attitude toward life. He believed in Fate, apparently, but he was not much concerned about it. He was interested in bringing order out of chaos; what could not be done did not concern him very much.[6] He was convinced that man should do his best while disregarding what is beyond the control of his ability, not that he should refrain from exerting himself and be dependent on Fate.

This brings us to the difference between Fate and *jen*. As a natural feeling of the human heart, *jen* is not only attainable but within the grasp of all. *Jen* is within one's own heart. Turn one's attention to oneself, and one is free from anxiety or fear, and so shall be happy. For it is in one's own heart, not in the external world, that one must seek for happiness. This is why Confucius said: "A wise man is free from doubts; a *jen* man, from anxiety; a brave man, from fear" (IX–28). And again: "A superior man is always happy; a common man is always sad" (VII–36). As to himself, he said:

> To eat only vegetables and drink only water, with bent arm for pillow: there can be happiness in such a life. Unrighteous wealth and honors are to me as wandering clouds (VII–15).
>
> I do not complain against Heaven, nor do I blame men. I study things on the lower level but my understanding penetrates the higher level. The one who knows me is Heaven! (XIV–37).

The second passage quoted above shows the wisdom of Confucius which makes him a great philosopher and a great sage. Because of his knowledge of Fate, he had no resentment against Heaven or men. As a man of *jen*, he was sure to have consideration of others, and out of this consideration he discovered the ideal of life—this is what is known as the "lower [moral] level" of life. Moreover, his ideal of life led to a search for the fundamental reality and ultimate truth of the universe —this is what is known as the "higher [transcendental] level" of life. As noted above, *jen* is the virtue through which the other virtues are to be attained and extended; it transcends the barriers of space and time. According to Confucius, to be *jen*-minded is not just to have a due regard for others; instead, to be *jen*-minded should involve a concern for the whole of humanity. A man of *jen* knows his moral responsibility in society and particularly in his relations with others, and also he is conscious of something above human society and relations—a larger reality, the Heaven, from which, for Confucius, man is derived. It is through the affirmation of Heaven that man will transcend himself and possess a meaning which is not limited to the human community. In this way, Confucius transcended the moral level. Fate, of which he spoke, may be interpreted either as the decrees of Heaven, or as the existent conditions of the universe, about which human beings can do little if anything. One's recognition of this is what Confucius called "knowing Fate." In this sense, Confucius' life-ideal is a vision of how *jen* is to be realized, through the knowledge of Fate. All these ideas seem simple and direct, yet they are profound and far-reaching. This is why Confucius claimed: "The one who knows me is Heaven!"

In this connection, we consider another passage in the *Lun Yü*:

> The Master said: "A resolute scholar and a man of *jen* will never seek to live at the expense of injuring *jen*. He would rather sacrifice his life in order to achieve *jen*" (XV–8).

For Confucius, life is decreed [7] and about it one can do relatively little. But as *jen* is within oneself, one who desires to seek it is sure to attain it. What is significant in Confucius' statement lies in his attempt to bring out the good that is in man, and not to put the good into man from without. We repeat, his great doctrine of *jen* is derived from his knowledge of Fate.

Since emphasis was thus placed on the knowledge of Fate, it was to be expected that Confucius would be free from four things: "He had no arbitrariness of opinion, no dogmatism, no obstinacy, and no egotism" (IX–4)—these things being incompatible with the doctrine of *jen*. Likewise, "Confucius never spoke of anomalies, prowess, violence or the supernatural" (VII–20). The reason is perhaps that these have to do with external forces, determined by Fate, beyond human effort. According to Confucius what man should do is to attend to *jen*—the right way of fulfilling oneself and developing oneself; that is, the ideal which embodies happiness and truth. We must remember that Confucius did not consider *jen* to be imposed upon man by an external force but rather something inborn in man. Man's own self is to be relied upon to have the free play of his judgment and .his good sense. Whatever force is involved is to come from within. For Confucius, learning is not just a matter of knowledge of things. It is something related to moral cultivation to fulfill and develop goodness in man. Confucius said: "It is man who can enlarge the *Tao* [Way], but not the *Tao* that can enlarge man" (XV–28). Therefore to learn is to enlarge the *Tao* through a process of moral cultivation, so as to attain *jen* and other related virtues.

As a natural feeling of the human heart, *jen* has to be expressed in man's exterior conduct in his relations with other men, maintaining order and harmony in society. For man can not live by himself, he has to relate to other men, and thus must follow appropriate rules governing human action and communication. Hence *li* (ritual)[8] is another important concept in the ethical system of Confucius. In the *Lun Yü* we read:

> Yen Yuan asked about *jen*, and the Master said: "Subdue oneself and return to *li*; this is *jen*. If a man can for one day subdue oneself and return to *li*, the world will accord him *jen*. For *jen* is to begin with oneself; does it begin in others?"
> "May I ask for an explanation?"
> "Look not at what is contrary to *li*; listen not to what is contrary to *li*; speak not what is contrary to *li*; and make no movement that is contrary to *li*."
> "Though I am slow-witted," said the disciple, "may I put this saying into practice!" (XII–1).

We must "know Fate" before we can seek for *jen*. We must "return to *li*" before we can achieve *jen*. While the knowledge of Fate is imperative in relation to the universe, the study of *li* is essential in relation to human society. This is why Confucius said:

> Who fails to know Fate can never be a superior man. Who fails to know *li* will have no means of standing firmly (XX–3).

It is evident that Confucius considered *li* as a means of establishing and adorning the right kind of conduct and attitude toward other men as well as toward spiritual beings. The importance of *li* for religious activities is obvious. As noted above, in early days, the dividing line between the dead and the living —as well as the divine and the human—was not sharp. They were indeed involved with each other. In this stage of religious belief, the ancient sage kings instituted *li* as a channel of guiding and facilitating the intercourse between this world and the other world, which was of course essential to the welfare of the whole humanity.

Furthermore, the ancient *li* was originally sacrificial and religious and later came to include all kinds of ceremonies and everything in connection with the proper conduct of a *chün-tzu* (an aristocrat). As a teacher, Confucius was keenly interested in the study of ancient *li*. However, it was the more complete and elegant *li* of Chou that especially captivated him. According to Confucius, the intrinsic value of *li* lies in its principles rather than in its appurtenances. He firmly insisted that a man without *jen* has nothing to do with *li* (III–3). Mere outward display disgusted him, as he protested: " 'It is *li*,' they say, 'it is *li*.' Does *li* mean no more than a display of jade and silk?" (XVII–11).

Thus Confucius upheld the spirit of ancient *li* against the ill-practice of the time, for he believed that the proper observance of *li* was essential to the development of goodness in an individual as well as in a society. *Li* for him was the restraining and refining force, creating the sense of balance and harmony in a man. Confucius said:

Reverence, if not regulated by *li*, becomes labored effort; prudence, if not regulated by *li*, becomes mere timidity; courage, if not regulated by *li*, becomes mere unruliness; frankness, if not regulated by *li*, becomes mere impudence (VIII-2).

As conceived here, the concept of *li* is "a kind of balance wheel of conduct," [9] guiding a way of life that avoids extremes, and a state of mind in which human reasoning and feeling reach perfect harmony. This is exactly what Confucius said: "Among the functions of *li*, the most valuable is that it establishes harmony. The excellence of the ways of ancient kings consists of this. It is indeed the guiding principle of all things, great and small" (I-12). In fact, the various forms of intellectual activity that make up the fabric of Chinese culture embrace and rest upon the concept of *li* as imparting harmony to human intercourse.

However, the significance of Confucius as a great philosopher lies in his attempt to transform the ancient *li* into a universal system of ethics. During the Chou period, as noted above, there was in religion an increased emphasis on ethics, accompanied by a lessening of the stress laid on mere ritual. This transition from ritual to ethical thinking greatly contributed to the process of ethicizing *li*. More important, in the hands of Confucius, *li*, originally a code of ritual for feudal lords, was now transformed into one of basic virtues in the great ethical system which has been important in Chinese culture ever since the time of Confucius. And it was by transforming the feudal conception of *li* into a universal ethical system that Confucius made a great contribution to Chinese thought.

Summing up, we find in the teachings of Confucius an ideal, a vision, a guiding principle and an insight into the meaning of life and the existence of the universe. But the keynote in his ethico-moral principles is "seeking-in-oneself"; that is, seeking what is one's mind. Faith in self-sufficiency for the individual is based on the assumption that man has "a genuine nature" [10] manifested in *jen*, acting in accordance with *li*, and based on the knowledge of Fate. Confucius put *jen* within the reach of every individual, without regard to the odds of the external world. This is why *jen* is the central idea of Confucius' philosophy.

Finally, some consideration must be given to Confucius' social and political philosophy. As "a follower of Chou," he must have seriously believed that a golden age of peace and prosperity had existed in the early Chou period, and that the social and political chaos was mainly due to the decline of the Chou feudal system with its moral and social values, the revival of which, consequently, was the urgent of all political efforts. Confucius felt that the first step toward the transformation of the chaotic world was to have everyone recognize and fulfill his own proper place, as illustrated in his famous doctrine of *cheng ming* (Rectification of Names).

Confucius had his reasons. In the *Lun Yü*, we read:

> Tzu Lu said: "The prince of Wei is awaiting you to take charge of his government. What will be your first measure?" The Master said: "It would be the rectification of names" (XIII–3).
> Then the Master continued: "If the names are not correct, then the words are inappropriate; when words are inappropriate, then things cannot be accomplished. . . . then rites and music will not flourish; . . . punishments will not be properly awarded; . . . and the people will not know how to put hand or foot. Hence a *chun-tzu* [superior man] designates what can be properly stated, and speaks what can be properly carried out. In what he says, there is nothing that is remiss" (ibid.).

In this sense, the doctrine of *cheng ming* is essentially the theory of "social status," the first principle of government. As a principle of social structure and social control, this doctrine makes for social order in China. *Cheng* means "rectification" and *ming* means "name." A name is a title that gives a man his definite status in society and defines his relationships with others. What is more important is that every man in social relationships implies certain responsibilities and duties. To rectify name (*cheng ming*) is to set up an objective standard of status by which one will behave in accordance with what the name of one's position implies. Thus on the principles of government, Confucius said:

> "Let the ruler be ruler, and the minister minister; let the father be father, and the son son" (XII–11).

For ruler, minister, father, and son are all the names which define social relationships, and those who bear these names must fulfill their responsibilities and duties accordingly. This is the implication of Confucius' doctrine of *cheng ming*.

The significance of Confucius as a political thinker lies in his endeavor to extend the doctrine of *cheng ming* to politics. In the *Lun Yü*, we read:

> When Chi K'ang-tzu (a powerful minister who had usurped the power in Lu) asked Confucius about the way to govern, Confucius said: "To govern (*cheng*) means to rectify. If you lead the people in rectitude, who will dare not be rectified?" (XII–17).

Thus Confucius firmly believed that the art of government consisted mainly in putting "every man in his place," but at the same time he insisted that this rectification should begin from the top. The same note is struck in his three basic principles of good government and orderly administration:

> [First], when the *Tao* [the way of government] prevails in the world, rites and music and punitive wars are originated by the emperor. . . . [Second], when the *Tao* prevails in the world, its policy is not in the hands of ministers. And [third], when the *Tao* prevails in the world, the people do not even discuss [government affairs] (XVI–2).

Confucius attributed to the ruler the highest degree of moral responsibility so as to set up a moral example for all those beneath him. For, asserted Confucius, if the ruler himself "desires what is good, the people will be good." "The prince (*chün-tzu*) is the wind, the common people (*hsiao-jen*) the grass, and the grass bends to the direction of the wind" (XII–19). But these political ideas, necessary at first for social order and political stability, later suffered much in the hands of politicians and emperors who used Confucius' great authority and standing to justify their autocratic rule.

The political thought of Confucius, as noted above, began as a means of bringing social order out of the chaos. If his political thought ended with the doctrine of *cheng ming*, which was codified in the relations between the ruler and the ruled, Confucius would be little more than an advocate of Chou feudalism, or a traditionalist, trying to reinforce the crumbling Chou culture. Thus looked at, how has he been in Chinese history placed in a most exalted position? Although Confucius said of himself as "a follower of Chou," he did not appear slavishly following it. On the contrary, he recognized that human institutions change and develop, and was ready to make or accept suitable changes. Thus he was not an indiscriminate but a selective "traditionalist." And again, Confucius deplored the political anarchy and condemned those who usurped the power and privilege of their superior, and so he seemed to be attached to the principle of legitimacy (*tsung-fa*). Nevertheless, he never attempted to restore the incompetent Chou line to power; on the contrary, he thought rather of building up a new central authority to take its place. This is what he meant when he said he hoped to create an "Eastern Chou." For many of his social and political ideas were indeed subversive of the status quo. Thus, though living in the feudal society of the sixth century B.C., he was able to transcend the limitations of his age and profession to develop a new ethical and political philosophy of his own, on the basis of the past cultural heritage.

We will not dwell on these ideas any further. What is important here is to recognize that Confucius thought of men as related in "one world—one family," so that all shared a common destiny which was to be guided by the cultivation and extension of one's goodness to the service of mankind. It is in this process of self-cultivation that one will attain a sense of purpose, a sense of destiny, or a sense of mission; it is also in this process that one will transcend one's ego, so as to enjoy an internal spiritual life. This was exactly what Confucius devoted his life to in his spiritual development and moral cultivation:

> Confucius said: "At fifteen, I set my mind on learning; at thirty, I stood firm [on *li*]; at forty, I had no doubts [about the purpose of life]; at fifty, I knew the Decree of Heaven (*T'ien-ming*); at sixty, I was ready to listen to it; and now, at seventy, I can follow my heart's desire, without transgressing [what is right]" (II–4).

As the ideas embodied in this passage have been discussed above, we need say no more than that. Confucius certainly gave us a concrete picture of a kind of ideal life. He also embodied the picture in his own life and showed us the way of emulating him. His ethical-moral principle has definitely molded the mentality and temperament of the Chinese. His basic concepts and terms, though interpreted in various ways, have remained vital until now. Moreover, though we deny the belief that Confucius could be anything like a savior of the modern world, his role as an inspiring and indefatigable teacher must remain crucial in history. Most important of all, his grand doctrine of *jen*, the acme of human relationship, is a great contribution to Chinese philosophy and to Chinese ethics.

3

The Idealistic School of Confucianism: Mencius

The dominant philosophy of China, as we have seen, has been Confucianism as founded by Confucius. It was developed by Mencius. There was good reason for this. Before the end of the Chou dynasty, several divisions of thought developed within the Confucian school. We have little information concerning the doctrines behind these divisions, but we know that Mencius and Hsün Tzu, both great champions of the Confucian school, gave widely different versions of what Confucius taught, which ultimately led to the formation of two rival camps, the idealistic and the realistic. We find, when we come to examine them, that the teachings of Mencius were akin to the whole rationale of Confucian thought, his temperament and philosophy being idealistic; while the major tenets of Hsün Tzu were obviously at odds with the Confucian orthodoxy, his temperament and philosophy being realistic.

His Life

Meng K'o, popularly known as Meng Tzu or Mencius, lived in the fourth century B.C., his approximate dates being 372–289 B.C. He was born in the small principality of Tsou, near Confucius' old home of Lu. He came of the artistocratic Meng Sun family of Lu. When the old order started to collapse, the Meng family left Lu for shelter in Tsou. Like Confucius, Mencius lost his father when he was only three years old. He was then brought up under the devoted care and instruction of Mother Meng, whose name is a household word even to this day.

When Mencius grew up, he studied under the pupils of Confucius' grandson, Tzu Ssu, and he was thus initiated into the great Confucian school. Early in life Mencius came to regard Confucius as his greatest inspiration. Like Confucius, he had a sense of mission, if only to suppress "perverse doctrines." With his winning eloquence, moral courage and deep conviction, Mencius popularized the doctrines of Confucius, at the same time zealously attacking the heterodox teachings of other schools, especially the followers of Mo Tzu and Yang Chu.[1]

Most of Mencius' working life was in the second half of the fourth century B.C., when the old China was beginning to disappear and great changes were in progress. This period, known in Chinese history as that of the Warring States (403–222 B.C.), was one of social disturbance, political instability, and intellectual anarchy. Mencius' attempts at political reform, therefore, met with no greater success than had those of his model.

Like Confucius, Mencius traveled for most of his life to offer advice to feudal lords on social and political reforms; also like Confucius, he failed to win royal support for his political doctrines and had to be satisfied with teaching and writing in his last years. And again like Confucius, Mencius was an educator par excellence; among his disciples he was greatly loved. As to himself, Mencius once said that there were three things in which he delighted, but to be sovereign of the world was not one of them; obtaining the young men of the finest talent in the world and educating them was his great delight (*Meng Tzu* VIIA–20). For his contributions in Confucianism, as well as for his defense of the great tradition, Mencius has been generally recognized as the greatest philosopher after Confucius, "the Second Sage."

The record of Mencius' teachings is found in the book that bears his name, the *Meng Tzu* (the *Book of Mencius*). This book consists of a series of discourses with his disciples and others, including ministers and feudal lords or kings, as most of them styled themselves. The *Meng Tzu* now ranks as one of the sacred "Four Books," the other three being the *Analects* (*Lun Yü*), the *Great Learning* (*Ta Hsüeh*), and the *Doctrine of the Mean* (*Chung Yung*). Compared with the ancient classics, the *Meng Tzu* excels particularly because of its interesting content and its beautiful and lucid style. Although the authenticity of Mencius' personal authorship has at times been questioned, the opinion, as stated in the *Shih Chi*, that Mencius "retired and, together with his disciple, Wan Chang, and others, put the *Shih* and *Shu* into order, transmitted the doctrines of Confucius, and composed the *Meng Tzu* in seven books" (ch. 74), has subsequently met with general acceptance. It is believed that at one time the complete works of Mencius consisted of eleven books, but only seven books have come down to us. The text, edited by Chu Hsi (A.D. 1130–1200), the preeminent philosopher of the Sung period, is divided into fourteen chapters.

His Thought

As an apostle of the Confucian school, Mencius naturally made *jen* the focal point of his thought. However, he claimed that, for the cultivation of moral character, *jen* should be coupled with *yi* (righteousness). For Confucius, *yi* is an important moral force that, together with *li*, guides and regulates one's conduct.[2] It was Mencius who gave *yi* the position of cardinal virtue to that of *jen*. As to the difference between *jen* and *yi*, Mencius said: "*Jen* represents the human heart; *yi* the human way" (the *Meng Tzu*, VA–11). In this light, *jen* is a natural feeling that comes from the human heart, whereas *yi* is the proper way to which one ought to conform. That is to say, *yi* involves a moral obligation, which is unconditional and absolute. In our community life, there are certain things which should be done for their own sake, because they are obligatory in themselves. If one does these things only because of other, nonmoral, considerations—say, as the means to achieve one's personal ends—one's action is no longer righteous, because one is then acting for profit and not for *yi*. Confucian scholars laid special emphasis on the distinction between profit and *yi*. Confucius said: "The superior man comprehends *yi;* the inferior man comprehend profits" (the *Lun Yü* TV–16). Mencius said: "One who rises at cockcrow and gives onself diligently to goodness is a follower of Shun [the sage king]. If one gets up at cockcrow and gives oneself to profit, one is merely a follower of Chih [the great robber]. Therefore the distinction between Shun and Chih lies between profit and goodness" (the *Meng Tzu* VIIA–25). This distinction Mencius considered to be paramount in moral importance. This is the reasoning used by Mencius in his opposition to the idea of utility. In his effort to develop the ideal of *yi*, Mencius made his chief contribution to Chinese thought and expressed his belief in the innate goodness of human nature.

Much controversy had arisen among the followers of Confucius as to the moral quality of human nature, and Mencius was the first to enunciate distinctly the doctrine that the nature of man inclines him to goodness and kindness. There were in Mencius' time three different theories on this subject. One, advanced by Kao Tzu with whom Mencius had many arguments, held that human nature was neither good nor bad. Another maintained that human nature could be either good or bad, depending upon circumstances. The third stated that the nature of some men was good while that of others was bad.

There is one passage from the *Meng Tzu* that serves as a general statement of the doctrine that man's nature is good:

> If left to follow its innate feelings, human nature will do good. This is what I mean by saying that human nature is good. If it becomes evil, it is not the fault of man's natural endowment.
>
> The feeling of compassion is common to all men; so is that

of shame and dislike; that of reverence and respect; and that of right and wrong. The feeling of compassion is *jen;* that of shame and dislike is *yi;* that of reverence and respect is *li;* and that of right and wrong is *chih* (wisdom). *Jen, yi, li,* and *chih* are not imposed upon us from without; they are inherent in our nature. Only we give them no thought. As the saying goes, "Seek and you will find them; neglect and you will lose them." [Men differ from one another]—some twice as much as others, some five times as much, and some incalculably more. It is because they cannot develop their innate endowment to the fullest extent. It is said in the *Shih* (Poetry): "Heaven produces the teeming multitude; all things are governed by proper principles. Abide by the nature of man, and all will love the virtue of goodness" (VIA–6).

This passage makes three salient points: first, man is good by nature and will naturally do what is good; second, man possesses four good feelings which imply four great virtues— *jen, yi, li,* and *chih;* third, men differ in the development of their innate goodness. Each of three points will be examined further.

One particular debate between Mencius and Kao Tzu illustrates Mencius' views on human nature:

Kao Tzu said: "Human nature is like the willow and *yi* like a cup or a bowl. To turn human nature into *jen* and *yi* is like turning the willow into cups and bowls."

To this Mencius replied: "Sir, can you, following the nature of the willow, make out of it the cups and bowls? Or must you deprive the willow of its nature in the process of making cups and bowls? If you must deprive the willow of its nature to make cups and bowls, then would you in like manner deprive man of his nature in the process of developing *jen* and *yi?* Your words, alas, would lead all in the world to regard *jen* and *yi* as calamity!" (VIA–1).

Indeed, Kao Tzu's analogy is unsound since the natural growth of the willow must be stopped in order to make cups and bowls out of it, while *jen* and *yi* are the development of the natural feelings that come directly from the human heart.

> Again, Kao Tzu said: "Human nature is like whirling water. Open an outlet to the east, and it flows to the east; open an outlet to the west, and it flows to the west. For human nature is indifferent to good or bad, just as water is indifferent to the east or to the west."
> Mencius rejoined: "Water will indeed flow indifferently to the east or west, but will it flow indifferently up or down? Human nature is disposed to goodness just as water tends to flow downward. There is no water but that it flows downward, and no man but he who shows tendency to be good. Now, by splashing water you may cause it to fly over your head; and by damming it, you may make it go uphill. But is this the nature of water? It is only an external force that causes it to do so. Likewise, when man is made to do what is not good, his nature is distorted in the same way" (VIA–2).

Moreover, Mencius saw human nature as confounded by the externals of life. He insistently maintained that human nature is originally good, but that it may become depraved through man's environmental influences. This, of course, does not allow us to say that human nature is not good. Mencius extended this idea to maintain that men by nature are the same, their differences being due to environment. He compared men to crops of barley that are alike but only so long as they are grown under identical circumstances (VIA–7).

However, it must be noted that while attention was thus focused on the goodness of human nature, Mencius did not fail to recognize that nurture could bring nature to its fruition and that environmental influences are important to the development of the individual. Mencius said:

> The ability possessed by man and not acquired through learning is innate ability. The knowledge possessed by man and not acquired through reflection is innate knowledge. Thus

every child, when he is carried in the arms, knows enough to love his parents. When he is grown up, he knows enough to respect his elder brothers. The love for one's parents is *jen*, and the respect for one's elders is *yi*—all these are feelings common to mankind in the world (VIIA-15).

Love and respect are innate feelings which are common to all men and are possessed by them without having to be learned. Just as from love emerges *jen*, so from respect emerges *yi*. For Mencius, love and respect indeed embody what is good in human nature. Therefore, the true end of life, Mencius believed, lies in the development and cultivation of the innate goodness.

When Mencius held that human nature is good, he meant that all men are born with an inclination toward goodness. As to the meaning of the term good, Mencius seemed to believe that the "good" is that which is in harmony with human nature. In his discussion of human nature, he pointed out that men's mouths agree in having the same relishes; their ears agree in enjoying the same sounds; their eyes agree in recognizing the same beauty" (VIA-7); from this illustration he reasoned that men's minds should approve similar principles; that is, "the principles of reason and *yi*." Hence Mencius concluded that "the principles of reason and *yi* are agreeable to our minds just as the flesh of grass-fed and grain-fed animals is agreeable to our mouths" (VIA-7).

For Mencius, as for Confucius, "the principles of reason and *yi*" are not imposed upon us from without; they are, on the contrary, inherent in human nature. Like Confucius, Mencius emphasized what is in oneself, as he said:

All things are already complete in oneself. There is no greater delight than to examine oneself and be sincere. If one acts with a vigorous effort at altruism (*shu*), *jen* is not far to seek, but right by one (VIIA-4).

There is good reason for this. Mencius said: "All men have a heart which cannot bear [to see the sufferings of] others" (IIA–6). This compassion leads to positive effort for the good of others. As an instance of this, Mencius said: "Now suppose that one suddenly sees a child about to fall into a well. One will immediately experience a feeling of alarm and distress. This is not so one will win the gratitude of the child's parents, not so he may seek the praise of one's neighbors and friends, nor because one is distressed at the child's cries" (IIA–6). The feeling of compassion, as well as feelings of shame and dislike, reverence and respect, and right and wrong, is a part of man's nature that distinguishes man from other creatures. In other words, that which makes man a man is the human heart.

This brings us to the question of why man should develop these innate feelings mentioned above. In the *Meng Tzu*, we read:

> Kung Tu Tzu asked: "We are all equally men; yet some become great and others become small. How is this?"
> Mencius said: "Those who follow the great part of themselves become great men, and those who follow the small part of themselves become small men." (VIA–15).

By "the great part" Mencius meant "the faculty of the heart," and by "the small part" he meant "the senses of sight and hearing." As to their distinction, Mencius pointed out: "The senses of sight and hearing do not think, but are obscured by [external] things. When the things come into contact with the senses, the latter will be led astray. But the faculty of the heart is to think. By thinking, one obtains what is good; without thinking, one fails to do so. This is what Heaven has conferred on us. Let a man first develop the great part of himself, and then the small part will not be able to deprive him of it. It is simply this which makes a great man." (VIA–15).

It is argued that the differences between men are not due to natural capacity endowed by Heaven. On the contrary, all men are fundamentally the same in their natural endowment. Hence Mencius said: "Yao and Shun [the ancient sage kings] were constituted just as other men are" (IVB–32). In fact, a sage is simply a man who has cultivated and developed his innate goodness to its full effectiveness. Mencius pleaded eloquently that cultivation could bring innate goodness to fruition and that environmental influences are important to the development of individuals. "Since all men have these four beginnings [innate feelings] in themselves," remarked Mencius, "let them know how to give them full development and completion. The result will be like fire that has begun to burn or a spring that has begun to find vent" (IIA–6).

Since attention was thus focused on the innate goodness, it was to be expected that Mencius would place his emphasis on the cultivation of moral character, so as to achieve, in particular, *jen* and *yi*. Mencius said:

> *Jen* is man's heart, and *yi* is man's path. Alas, for those who abandon the path and pursue it not! Alas, for those who lose the heart and seek it not! When men lose their fowls and dogs, they know to seek them. But they lose the heart they do not know how to seek it. The end of learning is nothing but the search for the lost heart (VIA–11).

To seek for the lost heart meant to try to recover one's original nature and preserve it. Mencius said: "That in which man differs from the birds and beasts is but slight. Ordinary men discard it, whereas superior men preserve it" (IVB–19). And again: "The great man is one who has not lost his child's heart" (IVB–12). This, Mencius felt, was the true end of human life; that is, to retain all the goodness that was originally in one's heart.

Even more important, Mencius was characteristically Confucian in his concern for the interplay among human beings. For both Confucius and Mencius, one's life is to be guided by the cultivation and perfection of goodness, not only in onself, but in everyone else to whom one is inevitably bound and related. Mencius once quoted the words of a wise man: "When Heaven produced the people, it decreed that those who are first in recognition should teach those who were later in recognition, and that those who were first in apprehension should teach those who were later in apprehension" (VA–7). All men are the same in their nature, but they are different in recognition and apprehension. This "recognition" or "apprehension" does not come spontaneously from the heart as an innate capacity. It is rather a result of one's conduct, in one's daily life, a result of the process of self-cultivation. For Mencius, it would not be enough to recover and preserve one's own innate goodness; one should develop and extend it, so that it would be a model of excellence for all.

> Treat the aged in my family as they should be treated, and extend this treatment to the aged of others' families. Treat the young in my family as they should be treated, and extend this treatment to the young of others' families (IA–7).

Mencius called this "extending one's good heart to include others," and he viewed it as the ultimate development of *jen* and *yi*.

Mencius' system stresses the importance of the individual, his improvement, and his perfection. The individual was to be relied upon, given the free play of his judgment and his good sense. Mencius said:

> When we get by our seeking and lose by our neglecting, our seeking is of use to getting, and the thing sought is something inherent in ourselves. When our seeking is in accord with the *Tao*, but the getting is determined by Fate, our seeking is of no use to getting, and the thing sought is something outside us (VIIA–3).

Therefore, what man should do is to seek what is in himself and to leave what is beyond his control to Fate. However, the fact that man is not able to control what is outside him does not make him imperfect; he is given by Heaven "the principles of reason and *yi*" within him, and in them he can find the "good." So Mencius said:

He who exerts his mind to the utmost knows his nature. He who knows his nature knows Heaven. To preserve one's mind and to nourish one's nature is the way to serve Heaven. To be without any double-mindedness regardless of premature death or longevity, but to cultivate one's person and wait [for Fate] is the way to establish one's Fate (VIIA–1).

Here is the essence of Mencius' theory of "waiting for Fate." As discussed in the preceding chapter, Heaven and Fate both exist in the universe, and about them human effort can do little. Mencius said: "That which is done without man's doing it, is from Heaven. That which happens without man's causing it to happen, is from Fate" (VA–6). What one should do is to exert oneself to the utmost in moral endeavor and disregard matters about which one can do little. At this point, Mencius was completely in harmony with Confucius' theory of "knowing Fate."

Mencius, however, carried his theory to, and even beyond, its logical conclusion. Thus he remarked: "All things are already complete in oneself" (VIIA–1). In other words, man is self-sufficient, if only he develops his inborn nature. This is why, as Mencius affirmed, everyone can be a sage. What is important here is to recognize that "seeking-in-oneself" involves the process of self-cultivation, leading to knowledge of the self in relation to other men and in relation to the universe: it is also in this process that a man not only knows Heaven, but also becomes one with Heaven, so that all distinctions between the self and non-self, between what is internal and what is external, are obliterated.

Moreover, Mencius' concept of innate goodness, which means, in essence, that all men are born morally equal, consists of the guiding principle of what he called "humane (*jen*) government." He said:

All men have a heart which cannot bear [to see the sufferings of] others. The early kings, having this "unbearing" (compassionate) heart, thereby had likewise an "unbearing" government (IIA–6).

An "unbearing" or "compassionate" government was in fact a humane government. True to the great tradition of the Confucian school, Mencius estimated highly the need of moral cultivation on the part of the people. He went, however, further than Confucius in his effort to take practical economic measures to assure the welfare of the people. The various discourses of Mencius about humane government, particularly addressed to the rulers of Wei, Ch'i, and T'eng, consist mainly of two major functions of a state: first, that of enriching the people generally, of improving their overall welfare; second, that of educating the people in ceremonial rites, in social order and in national loyalty.

Since Mencius was much concerned with the welfare of the people, his economic reforms largely consisted of land tenure, reduction of taxes, and what might be called "old age pension" (*yang lao*, "nourishing the aged"). As to the land tenure, Mencius stressed that "the first thing toward humane government must be land division and demarcation" (IIIA-3). As far as we know, in early times, all land, which belonged to the feudal lords of the various states, was parcelled out to the local peasants, who paid about a tenth of its produce as the annual rent. In the *Meng Tzu*, we read:

> Each square *li* ³ of land should be divided into nine plots, the whole containing nine hundred *mou*.⁴ The central plot is the public field, and the eight households, each owning a hundred-*mou* farm, cultivate the public field in common. Not till public work is finished, may they resume to attend their private affairs. This is the way of keeping the country men distinct [from their overlords] (IIIA-3).

This is known as the *chien-t'ien* (well-field) system,⁵ a form of cooperative farm. Mencius claimed the communal ownership of property under the *chien-t'ien* system, as he interpreted this supposedly ancient institution. Whether this egalitarian system was actually practiced in ancient times is questionable, but it obviously provided an equitable justification for his land reform.

With his goal of people's welfare in mind, Mencius also opposed the oppressive taxation of the time, especially burdensome because of the need for financing the ceaseless wars among the feudal lords. He recognized the necessity for taxation but aimed at reducing the heavy taxation on peasants, thereby ameliorating their living conditions. He cited three methods that had been or were then practiced: the Hsia tribute (*kung*) system, the Yin (Shang) mutual aid system, and the Chou share (*chih*) system. "But, in every case, the actual amount [of tax] was one-tenth [of the produce]. The share system [of Chou] means mutual division, while the aid system [of yin] means mutual dependence" (IIIA–3). Contrasted with the two systems and utterly condemned by Mencius was the tribute system of Hsia, in which each household had to pay a fixed tribute of grain, determined by the average yield of the land he tilled. As to the Hsia system, Mencius said:

> In the good years, when the grain lies in abundance, much can be taken without being oppressive, but only a small amount is taken. Whereas in the bad years, when the produce is not enough even to pay for the manuring, the fixed amount must be taken. The sovereign, as a parent to the people, causes them to toil hard all the year round, and yet they are not able to feed their parents. Then they proceed to borrow to make up the deficiency, with the result that the old people and children are found dying in the ditches and canals; wherein is he a parent to the people? (IIIA–3).

For the same reason, Mencius advocated to lighten levies on marketable goods, to abolish tolls and duties at the frontier passes, and to conscript the peasant's labor only at slack agricultural seasons. Most important of all, Mencius instituted what we might call old age pensions, as well illustrated in the following passages:

> If the seasons for farming are not interfered with, there will be more grains than can be consumed. If closed-meshed

nets are not allowed in the pools and lakes, there will be more fish and turtles than can be consumed. If the axes and hatchets are brought to the forest only at the proper time, there will be more timber than can be used. When the people have more grain, fish and turtle than they can eat, and more timber than they can use, they will be able to feed the living and bury the dead without any undue worry. To ensure this for his people marks the beginning of the "kingly sway" (*wang tao*).

Let the homesteads of five *mou* be planted with mulberry, and all persons over fifty may have silk to wear. Let proper seasons be not neglected in the breeding of poultry, pigs, dogs, and swine, and all persons over seventy may have meat to eat. Let a farm of a hundred *mou* not be robbed of its labor at the time [proper for its farming], and a family of several mouths will stave off the pangs of hunger. Let attention be paid to teaching in schools, with special regard to filial piety and fraternal love, and gray-haired men will not be seen on the roads bearing heavy loads. No ruler under whom the aged have silk to wear and meat to eat, and the common people suffer neither from hunger nor cold, has ever failed to be a [true] king (IA–3).

In the above passages, Mencius made it obvious that the economic welfare of the people was a necessary foundation of political stability, and therefore he attributed to the government and eventually to the ruler himself the highest degree of responsibility to provide for the material needs of the people.

As far as education was concerned, Mencius merely pointed out that moral education and good government go hand in hand. Mencius once said:

Kindly words do not touch so profoundly as kindly deeds. Likewise, good government does not hold people so firmly as moral education. For good government produces the people's awe, while moral education inspires their love. Good government gains the people's wealth, while moral education gains their hearts (VIIA–14).

Thus Mencius believed that the people should be well fed, warmly clad, and comfortably lodged, but he also advocated that they should be properly educated. In the same passages in which he advocated land reform, he proposed the establishment of a system of public schools, for the purpose of "making known the principles of governing human relations" (IIIA–3). But Mencius told us little about these schools save the mention of the various names by which they had been known in the past.

Viewed in this light, the way of humane government, as taught by Mencius, was fundamentally a question of political economy, the key to which was the amelioration of the people's livelihood. Here we find that Mencius' political principle was a departure from Confucius' esteem for moral character over the material needs. There are good reasons for this. First, hungry people cannot be expected, Mencius asserted, to be moral. "The way of [governing] the people is thus: If they have a certain means of livelihood, they will maintain a stead-fast heart. If they have no certain means of livelihood, they cannot maintain a steadfast heart. Without a steadfast heart, they are likely to abandon themselves to all manner of de-pravity" (IIIA–3). And again: "Therefore, when an enlight-ened ruler regulates the livelihood of the people, he makes sure that they will have enough to serve their parents and to support their wives and children. . . . Thus he urges them on toward goodness, and the people will follow him readily. But now the livelihood of the people is so regulated that they do not have enough to serve their parents or to support their wives and children. . . . Under such circumstances, they are only trying to save themselves from death; what leisure have they to cul-tivate *li* and *yi?*" (IA–7).

And secondly, political philosophy reflects the political cir-cumstances of its author. Living in the midst of warfare, Men-cius must have been especially impressed by the desperate con-dition of the people. He once said: "There has never been a time when people suffered more from an oppressive govern-ment " (IIA–1). "When wars are fought over territory, the slain fill the countryside. When wars are fought over citadels, the slain fill the citadels. This might well be called leading on the land to devour human flesh" (IVA–14). It was the actual state of affairs in his time that led him to lay a major stress on economics for the relief of the people's plight. Mencius, as a great champion of Confucian tradition, never intended to eschew Confucius' teachings. But as a great political philosopher, Mencius was, as we have seen, far more specific and advanced than his predecessor in his principles of government. Thus, for him it was not enough to say that people should be made prosperous and then educated.[6] Rather, he expounded his beliefs in the specific areas mentioned above, such as the *chien-t'ien* system of farming, the abolition of market taxes and frontier levies, etc. The implementation of these indigenous economic measures gave Mencius a distinct sense of independence from Confucius.

We will not dwell on these ideas any further. Mencius certainly gave us a system of ethico-political doctrines, and told us the way of attaining it. His faith in such an idealistic state of affairs becoming a reality was based on the assumption that human nature was good and Heaven would throw its weight on the side of the virtuous man. Therefore, for Mencius, the ultimate goal of life is goodness, and the final objective, for him, is man in his perfection, the great man. This ideal of the man of perfection is thus stated in the *Meng Tzu*.

> He who dwells in the broad house of the universe, stands firm on the right place of the universe, and walks in the great way of the universe; he who, if successful, walks along with the people, and if unsuccessful, walks in the way all alone; he whom wealth and honor cannot corrupt, poverty and obscurity cannot move, threats and violence cannot subdue—he it is who may be called a great man (IIIB–2).

A great man, being regarded as a model of the human society, requires moral character and the sense of responsibility to humanity or the Tao, which he must protect even at the cost of life. So Mencius said: "Life, I like, and *yi*, I also like. If I cannot have both of them, I shall give up life in order to choose *yi*" (VIA–10). Here again, Mencius was completely in harmony with the teachings of Confucius with regard to the purpose of human life. Just as Confucius spoke of one who "would give up life in order to acheve *jen*" (the *Lun Yü*, XV–8), so Mencius would "give up his life in order to choose *yi*." In this sense, the two sages both were men of faith and religious sentiment; though Confucianism is not essentially a religion. A firm belief in the goodness of human nature is their religious faith; a complete devotion to the ends of human life is their religious spirit.

4

The Realistic School of Confucianism: Hsün Tzu

Mencius and Hsün Tzu (*fl.* 298–238 B.C.), as mentioned previously, represented two rival schools of thought—the idealistic and the realistic—and developed Confucianism in two directions. Just as Mencius followed Confucius' humanistic ideas in his emphasis on *jen* and *yi* as guiding principles of his system, so Hsün Tzu attached importance to ceremonial codes (*li*) and social institutions as means to attain social and political progress. Nevertheless, the division in the Confucian school should not be taken so clear-cut and complete as it sounds. We must keep in mind that both Mencius and Hsün Tzu revered the Sage as their master and imitated him as a model. Both subscribed to and enhanced the sage-ideal and the great virtues attached to the superior man. We must also remember that, coming at the end of the Chou period, Hsün Tzu had the benefit, as well as the impact, of a variety of thinkers and teachers. Hsün Tzu's teachings not only expressed the ideas of Confucius but also incorporated the best thought of other schools, such as Taoism, Legalism, and Mohism. He summarized for posterity the intellectual achievement of the ancients in the most creative age. That Hsün Tzu was not in complete compliance with the Confucian orthodoxy, as founded by Confucius and developed by Mencius, should not surprise us.

His Life

Hsün Tzu, whose name was K'uang, also known as Ch'ing, was a native of the state of Chao, on the edge of modern Shansi, through which the Hans, Turks, and Mongols invaded China. While the dates of his birth and death are not precisely known, it seems probable that he lived to witness the Period of Warring States (402–221 B.C.) reaching its climax, in which the state of Ch'in conquered all its rival states and unified China for the first time. He was strongly influenced by the turmoil of this period and reflected it in his writings.

Not much is known of the philosopher's life. In his early years, he seems to have been in the state of Yen. The king there was struck by Hsün Tzu's talents but hesitated to take him into his service. Then, Hsün Tzu devoted himself to academic research and teaching until the age of fifty, when he was invited to the state of Ch'i, the great intellectual center of the age. There he was highly honored as an eminent scholar. He appears to have been given office at the court, for he "acted three times in the capacity of a libation officer at the great temple sacrifice." [1] But the scholars and courtiers, in order to check his ascendancy in the court, felt it necessary to counteract his influence and spread scandal against him. As a result of this, Hsün Tzu resigned his post and then went to the state of Ch'u. Through the recommendation of Ch'un Sun-chun, the prime minister of Ch'u, Hsün Tzu was appointed the chief magistrate of Lan-ling. The death of the prime minister led him to abandon his political life, although he never again left the state of Ch'u.

In Lan-ling, Hsün Tzu surrounded himself with a group of young men, some of whom rose to eminence in letters and politics. Among his disciples, the two most famous were Li Ssu, prime minister of Ch'in, and Han Fei, a distinguished Legalist, both of whom stood for firm and authoritative government and for drastic regulations to guarantee social order. Such political and intellectual trends as these might account to some extent for his "tough-minded" realism, in opposition to the "tender-minded" idealism of Mencius.[2]

His manner of life as a social and political reformer was much like that of Confucius. At first he sought to effect his object by taking part in politics and setting an example of good government, as well as by giving instruction to young men. But he met with little success in politics, though he retained his belief in man.

The teaching and personality of Confucius constituted the supreme intellectual impulse of his life and inspiration of his thought. Of Confucius, he said:

> Confucius was human-hearted and sagacious, and was not blinded. Therefore his learning was so comprehensive that he was worthy to be ranked with the early [sage] kings. His school embraced the whole of the Chou system, and put it into practice without blindness to the whole. Hence his virtue was equal to that of Duke Chou; his fame was on a par with that of the Three Kings.[3] This was the blessing of being free from blindness (the *Hsün Tzu* ch. XXI).

Hsün Tzu lived in an age when "the hundred schools" of thought developed in a fantastic heterodoxy that threatened to undermine orthodox Confucianism. For this reason, like Mencius, he had to uphold the teachings of Confucius by attacking those of other schools. In an essay entitled "Against the Twelve Masters " (the *Hsün Tzu* ch. VI), he launched an all-out attack against his contemporaries, including not only rival philosophers such as the Taoists, the Mohists, and the Logicians, but also such prominent Confucians as Tzu Ssu (Confucius' grandson) and Mencius. In the same essay we read:

> There were men who generally followed the early kings but did not know their basic systems. Yet their abilities were various, their ambition was great, their experience and knowl-

edge were many-sided and diverse. Based on ancient traditions, they developed theories which were called the Five Elements.[4] Their views were peculiar, contradictory and without standards; obscure and without illustrations; confined and without explanations. They exalted their statements, saying: "These are true sayings of the former superior man [Confucius]." Tzu Ssu began it, and Mencius followed. The ignorant scholars of the world welcome it and did not know that it was false. They accepted it and passed it on, thinking that because of this, Confucius and Tzu Lu [a disciple of Confucius] would carry authority with later generations. This was the fault of Tzu Ssu and Mencius (ch. VI).

Of course conflict between Hsün Tzu and Mencius split the Confucian school. Among the Confucians, Hsün Tzu has not enjoyed high favor, and Mencius has been regarded as in the direct line of the transmission of Tao from Confucius. Hsün Tzu's work was not elevated to the position of a Confucian classic, and no commentary had ever been written on it until recently. Still Hsün Tzu's influence on the development of Confucianism was tremendous, and, Hsün Tzu was, indeed, one of the most brilliant thinkers the world has ever produced. As long as the intellectual history of China is studied, his rationalism and realism, his logical theories, his stress on the ceremonial codes (*li*) and legal institutions, and his views on education and fallacies of the various philosophical schools will always merit special attention.

The teachings of Hsün Tzu are preserved in a book bearing his name and supposed to have been written by himself, but some sections of it were either written by his students, or added to it by Confucians of the Han period. The book originally consisted of three hundred and twenty-two essays, but after being edited and condensed, in the standard edition of the *Hsün Tzu* there are only thirty-two essays. Unlike the *Meng Tzu*, which consists of dialogues, the *Hsün Tzu*, as a series of well-organized essays, is more logical in reasoning and more exquisitely written.

His Thought

Hsün Tzu differed fundamentally from Mencius. On the nature of man, he rejected Mencius' doctrine that human nature is good; the political turmoil of his period convinced Hsün Tzu that man by nature is evil. In the conception of Heaven, Hsün Tzu leaned far in the direction of the Taoists' impersonal, naturalistic *Tao*. For him, Heaven was not a moral principle or a spiritual entity, as conceived by Mencius, but the unvarying law of natural phenomena. The belief in the goodness of human nature follows from an idea of a moral-spiritual Heaven, whereas the belief in evil human nature suggests an indifferent Heaven. In this and other respects, the two great philosophers, as they differed in views and temperament, have been compared with Aristotle and Plato respectively. Of human nature, Hsün Tzu said:

> The nature of man (*hsing*) is evil; his goodness is acquired training (*wei*). Now man, by his nature, is born, first, with a desire for gain. If this desire is followed, strife and rapacity will result, whereas courtesy and compliance disappear. Second, man is born with envy and hate. If these tendencies are followed, injury and cruelty will abound, whereas loyalty and good faith disappear. Third, man is born with the lusts of the ear and eye, leading to the love of sound and beauty. If these lusts are followed, lewdness and disorder will spring up, whereas *li* and *yi*, together with good manners, disappear. Hence, if man gives full rein to his nature and follows his passions, there will be assuredly strife and rapacity, leading to a breach of order and confounding reason, culminating in violence. Only under the civilizing influence of teachers and laws, and the guidance of *li* and *yi*, does man conform to courtesy and compliance, observe good manners, and submit to order. From all this, it is evident that the nature of man is evil, and his goodness is acquired training (the *Hsün Tzu*, ch. XXIII).

Thus Hsün Tzu stressed the distinction between "original nature *(hsing)*" and "acquired training *(wei)*." In the *Hsün Tzu,* we read:

> That which cannot be learned or worked for, [but rests with Heaven], is what I call original nature. That which can be either learned or worked for, and rests with man, is what I call acquired training. This is the distinction between original nature and acquired training (ch. XXIII).

Hsün Tzu elaborated this distinction further:

> Man's nature is the crude material of the original; what belongs to acquired training is the accomplishment and refinement brought about by culture and *li.* Without original nature there would be nothing to which we could add acquired training. But without acquired training, original nature could not be beautiful of itself (ch. XIX).

It is evident that human nature is a congenital quality of man capable of being improved. But "acquired training" is the deliberate work of man which enables him not merely to improve himself but to restrain the evil impulses of human nature. For instance, "crooked wood needs to undergo steaming and bending by the carpenter's tools; only then is it straight. Blunt metal needs to undergo grinding and whetting; only then is it sharp" (ch. XXIII). Likewise, the evil inherent in human nature needs to be rectified by "the influence of teachers and laws and the guidance of the codes of ceremonies *(li)* and righteousness *(yi)*" *(ibid.)*; only then will all be in accord with goodness.

Along with his emphasis on the importance of "acquired training," Hsün Tzu recognized the importance of environmental influences in the development of the individual. He offered the following illustration:

> In the south there is a bird, called the *Meng-ch'iu,* which makes its nest with feathers, weaves it with hair, and attaches

it to reeds. When the wind blows, the reeds snap, the eggs break, and the birdlets die. The nest is well-made, but the disaster is due to the reeds to which it is attached. In the west there is a plant, called the *She-kan*. Its stalk is only four inches long, but it grows on a high mountain, overlooking a deep gulf. Its stalk does not grow longer, but the advantage lies in the location where it grows. Raspberry vines growing among hemp keep straight without being supported; white sand in black mud becomes black with the mud. The root of Lan-huai [a fragrant plant] is as fragrant as the Chih [also a fragrant plant]. But if it is soaked in manure, gentlemen will not come near it, nor will the common people like it. It is not because its quality is not excellent, but because it is soaked in manure. Hence, for his dwelling-place, the superior man should carefully select a proper community; on his travel study he should go to the real scholar. He might thereby keep himself away from the heretical and the depraved, and associate himself with the orthodox and the upright (ch. I).

Hsün Tzu's reasoning was based on the theory that man was endowed at birth with intelligence and that this intelligence enabled man to transform the crude materials of his nature into a mature, refined personality through the process of cultivation. Hence what one needed, as Hsün Tzu constantly insisted, was constant practice in the "accumulation of *li* and *yi*," which would bring one "to a state of moral order."

Mencius recognized the importance of environment and put emphasis on its function in the cultivation of one's nature. However, the agreement between the two philosophers ends there. According to Hsün Tzu, the ultimate objective of cultivation was not merely to improve human nature, but also to counteract its evil impulse, so that man might acquire some goodness to transform his evil nature. This sort of interpretation could not be accepted by the orthodox Confucian philosophy. To both Confucius and Mencius, cultivation was to bring out the good that was in man, and not to put the good into man who had been rectified of his evil nature.

The difference between Hsün Tzu and Mencius "might be

summarized as one of externity versus internality of relations." [5] Since Hsün Tzu viewed human nature as essentially evil, it was to be expected that he would consider all knowledge, wisdom and values as acquired by the individual from without. He therefore stressed conformity and observance. In place of *jen* (the natural compassion of human heart), he introduced a code of ceremonial (*li*)[6] and legal institutions as the most effective means of combating the evil in human nature. Mencius, on the other hand, began with the individual endowed with "four innate good-feelings," which, if properly cultivated, would grow and ripen in the mind. To Mencius, "to cultivate" meant to "draw out" the good which was inherent in ourselves. This was an important point in which Hsün Tzu was not in compliance with Confucian orthodoxy.

Another important tenet on which Hsün Tzu diverged from Confucius and Mencius was his conception of Heaven. The religious idea of the early Chinese, which culminated in their belief in the "Mandate of Heaven" as clearly expressed in the *Shu Ching*, had been significantly modified during the period between Confucius and Hsün Tzu. As we know, Confucius seemed to be equivocal about supernatural beings, and though he glorified Heaven as supreme in providence he seldom openly spoke of his faith. To Mencius, Heaven was at times a divine entity and at times a moral principle. Now to Hsün Tzu, Heaven was a natural phenomenon, pursuing its course quite unconcerned about human affairs. In his chapter "On Heaven" (ch. XVII), Hsün Tzu said:

> Heaven conducts itself with constant regularity. It did not prevail on account of [the virtue of] Yao [a sage-king], nor would it cease to prevail because of [the wickedness of] Chieh [a tyrant]. Respond to it with peace and order, and blessings will result. Respond to it with disorder, and calamity will result.

And again:

Does Heaven decide whether order or chaos will prevail? I say: The sun and moon, stars and planets were the same in the time of Yü [a sage-king] as in that of [the tyrant] Chieh. However, Yü brought about order, whereas Chieh brought about chaos. Hence Heaven does not decide whether order or chaos will prevail (*ibid.*).

This was Hsün Tzu's view of Heaven as nature running its own course, oblivious of human affairs and unaffected by them. Heaven did not prevail on account of the virtue of the sage-king, nor would it cease to prevail because of the wickedness of the tyrant. Indeed, Hsün Tzu was convinced that Heaven, as a natural phenomenon, was no source of blessing, and therefore he insisted that it was man himself, and not Heaven, upon whom depended his own life and also all prosperity or calamity that came upon him. Thus he said:

When the fundamentals of living are built up and used economically, then Heaven cannot bring poverty. When the people's sustenance is provided for and their labor is employed in keeping with the seasons, then Heaven cannot inflict sickness. When the *Tao* is followed and is not deviated from, then Heaven cannot send misfortune. Therefore, flood and drought cannot cause a famine; the [winter's] cold or the [summer's] heat cannot cause illness; and devils or demons cannot cause disaster (*ibid.*).

Moreover, Hsün Tzu raised a protest against supernaturalism, insisting that cosmic anomalies or prodigious signs did not portend disasters. In the same chapter on Heaven, there is an illustrative passage:

When stars fall or trees groan, all the people become afraid and ask: "What is this?" I would say: This is but natural disturbance caused by the modification of Heaven and Earth and the mutation of the *yin* and *yang*—all these are uncommon events. We may marvel at them, but we should not fear them. For there is no age which has not experienced eclipses of the sun and moon, unseasonable rain and wind, or the occasional appearance of strange stars. If the ruler is enlightened and government is equitable, even though these phenomena should all occur at once, no harm would be done. If the ruler is unenlightened and the government is bent on evil, although none of these phenomena should occur, it would still be of no avail (ch. XVII).

The real significance of Hsün Tzu as a great thinker lies in his attempt to eliminate superstition from the early Chinese thought. However, though he derided the demons of mythology, he did not seek to suppress or transform the popularly accepted customs and ceremonies, such as sacrifices, especially those to ancestors. These ceremonial and sacrificial practices, according to Hsün Tzu, were no longer religious, but simply ornamental or symbolic. In his rejection of supernatural beliefs and cosmic speculations, Hsün Tzu succeeded in separating religion from philosophy and making man independent of Heaven. This was indeed a very laudable undertaking and it contributed to the growing agnostic element in Chinese thought.

Since Hsün Tzu diverged so much in his fundamental outlook on Heaven and human nature from the teachings of Confucius and Mencius, how could he have maintained that he was a Confucianist? The answer is to be found in his criticism of the rival schools of philosophy, particularly those of Mo Tzu,[7] Hui Tzu,[8] and Chuang Tzu.[9] Here we shall find the essence of Hsün Tzu's philosophy. Hsün Tzu agreed, with most of the early thinkers, that there was a single absolute truth (the *Tao*) existing for all eternity and evidenced in all things. However, he maintained that most of the philosophical schools had concentrated on one aspect of the *Tao*, failing to know the whole truth. For instance:

> Mo Tzu was blinded by utility and did not know the value of culture. . . . Hui Tzu was blinded by words and did not know reality. Chuang Tzu was blinded by heaven [nature] and did not know man (ch. XXI).

There is good reason for this:

> From the point of view of utility, the *Tao* is nothing but to seek profit. . . . From the point of view of words, the *Tao* is nothing but argumentation. From the point of view of heaven, the *Tao* is nothing but *laissez-faire* (*Ibid.*).

"Those with partial knowledge," concluded Hsün Tzu, "perceive only one aspect of the *Tao*, but fail to know its totality" (*Ibid.*). On the other hand, Confucius, human-hearted and sagacious, "was not blinded and therefore comprehended the *Tao*" (*Ibid.*). Hence, according to Hsün Tzu, the teachings of Confucius were superior to those of all other schools because they were more comprehensive and complete.

As mentioned above, Hsün Tzu absorbed into his own system not only the ideas of Confucius but also the best thought of the other philosophical schools, such as the Mohist, the Dialecticians, and the Taoists. His system has been called the philosophy of culture. We know that value comes from culture, and culture itself is the achievement of man, including all rites and institutions. Since emphasis was thus placed on the cultural achievement, it followed that Hsün Tzu recognized the importance of a social organization in which all shared in the undertaking of its purpose and the enjoyment of its benefits. So Hsün Tzu said:

> What a hundred workmen accomplish goes for the nourishment of one single individual. Yet one able man cannot be skilled in more than one line, and one man cannot hold two offices simultaneously. If people live together and do not serve one another, there will be poverty. If they live together, but are without social distinctions, there will be strife. Poverty is a misfortune and strife is a calamity. To rescue people from misfortune and calamity, there is nothing like making social distinctions clear and forming a social organization (ch. X).

This explains why men must have a social organization, with clear norms of conduct to be observed and restrictions to be complied with. These are the ceremonials (*li*), the control of a well-ordered society. On the origin of *li*, Hsün Tzu said:

> Whence does *li* arise? I say: Man is born with desires. When these desires are not satisfied, he cannot but pursue their satisfaction. When the pursuit is carried on without restraint or limit, there cannot but be strife. When there is strife, there is chaos. When there is chaos, there is dissolution. The early kings were disgusted at this chaos, and so they instituted *li* and *yi*, to put an end [to this chaos], so that man's desires might be nourished and their pursuit be gratified. In this way desires would not be frustrated by things, nor would things be used by desires; these two should mutually balance each other and so continue to exist. This is from whence *li* arises (ch. XIX).

Here is the function of *li*, serving to determine proper limits and thus restrain the desires. Man's desires are thus regulated, so as to assure the material welfare of the society as a whole. This line of reasoning, like that of Mo Tzu, is utilitarian. But Hsün Tzu went further. The function of *li* was not just to regulate human desires; it was to beautify and refine human emotions. Thus Hsün Tzu said:

> It is through *li* that love and hatred are tempered, and joy and anger are appropriate. *Li* causes the lowly to be obedient and those on high to be illustrious. One who holds to *li* is not confused in the midst of multifarious changes; one who deviates therefrom is lost. Is not *li* the culmination of culture? (*ibid.*)

Mo Tzu, on the other hand, held that human emotions, on the utilitarian basis, were valueless, and so should be repressed. At this point, Hsün Tzu denounced Mo Tzu as blinded by utility to the detriment of culture. So in justifying mourning and sacrificial rites, which Mo Tzu and his followers denounced as extravagant, Hsün Tzu gave these practices new interpretations and read into them new ideas. He regarded these elaborate rites as the expression of man's affection and love for the dead.

They were indeed useful. They fulfilled human needs, not of the dead but of the living.

As mentioned above, there was a School of Names, which taught the theory of knowledge and the art of dialectic. These dialecticians debated such propositions as "A white horse is not a horse," "Fire is not hot," and "An egg has feathers." As the leading Confucianist of his day, Hsün Tzu propounded his Rectification of Names (*cheng ming*) theory in order to combat this "erring school of thought." The term "Rectification of Names" was originated by Confucius and its application was originally limited to ethics. But Hsün Tzu's theory was not so confined. It was closely associated with the logical principles of theoretical knowledge.

As to the origin and purpose of names, Hsün Tzu said:

> Names were made in order to denominate actualities—on the one hand so as to distinguish the superior from the inferior, and, on the other hand, to discern similarities and differences (ch. XXII).

Names originated partly for social differentiation and partly for logical differentiation.

As to the logical use of names, let us summarize briefly what Hsün Tzu elaborated in the chapter (XXII) on "the Rectification of Names":

1. Same names are given to those that are of the same kind, and different names to those that are of different kinds.

2. A simple name is given to what is simple, and a compound name to what is compound. For instance, "horse" is a simple name. If the horse is white, then a compound name—in this case, "white horse"—is applicable.

3. A common name is given to those that have a common characteristic, applying to both the simple and compound name. For instance, "animal" is a common name for both "horse" and "white horse."

4. "Great General Name" is given to those that are denominated by the extension of "things." For instance, the

term *things* is a great general name that includes "animals, plants, and metals" and many similar items.

5. "Great Specific Name" is given to those that are denominated by the intension of "things." For instance, the term "birds and beasts" is a great specific name, for "birds" excludes "animals" and *vice versa*.

In view of the last two points, it is evident that Hsün Tzu had a clear conception of the logical method for the denomination of things. The general name is the product of the synthetic process of reasoning, while the specific name is that of an analytic process. On the basis of these five principles concerning terminology, Hsün Tzu demolished the confusing propositions of the dialecticians and denounced them as blinded by words to the neglect of actualities. He accused them of playing word games with philosophy.

Finally, there was another important rival school of thought known as Taoism, standing for nature and opposing all human institutions. Hsün Tzu had to combat it in order to defend the great Confucian tradition. Let us first quote a passage from his essay concerning Heaven (ch. XVII):

> Hence one who understands the distinction between Heaven and man may be called a perfect man. To accomplish without any action and to obtain without effort, this is what is meant by the office of Heaven. This being the case, although [the Way of Heaven] is deep, the perfect man will not deliberate over it. Although it is great, he will not devote his effort to it. And although it is exquisite, he will not scrutinize it. This is what is meant by not contesting with Heaven.

That is Hsün Tzu's argument for clear distinction between Heaven and man—distinction that culminated in the theory of the "division of Heaven and man." It is in this theory that man has the same importance in the universe as Heaven and Earth. As Hsün Tzu said:

> Heaven has its seasons; Earth has its wealth; man has his government. This is how man is able to form a triad [with

Heaven and Earth]. If he should neglect his own part in this triad and put all his hope in [Heaven and Earth with which he forms] the triad, he is making a grave mistake (*ibid.*).

According to Hsün Tzu, the three powers of the universe—Heaven, Earth, and man—each have their own functions. So he said:

> The fixed stars make their rotations; the sun and moon alternately shine; the four seasons follow one another; the *yin* and *yang* go through their mutations; the wind and rain spread over all things. The myriad things acquire their harmony, and thus grow; each thing gets its nourishment and thus achieves its full development. We do not see the cause of these occurrences, but we do see their results. This is what is called spirit. We all know how they achieve their full development, but we do not know their invisible process. This is what is called Heaven. It is only the sage who does not seek to know Heaven (*ibid.*).

In his naturalistic interpretation of Heaven, Hsün Tzu came closer to Taoism than the Confucian school to which he belonged. For he believed with Chuang Tzu that Heaven was no more than the order of nature, and that all changes in the universe (such as the movement of stars, the alternation of the sun and moon, the succession of the seasons, the mutation of the *yin* and *yang*, and the distribution of the wind and rain) were operations of this order. Because of this order, the sage did not seek to know Heaven; but, instead, he had to make his own effort for self-improvement and adjustment with Heaven and Earth, so as to be able to control Heaven's seasons and to utilize Earth's resources. In this way, man can form a triad with Heaven and Earth. Therefore he said:

> You exalt Heaven and think about it:
> Why not heap up [its wealth] and regulate it?
> You obey Heaven and praise it:
> Why not control its mandate and use it?

> You look on the seasons and wait for them:
> Why not respond to them and make use of them?
> You rely on things to increase of themselves:
> Why not put forth your ability and multiply them?
> You consider things as things:
> Why not attend to them so as not to lose them?
> You admire how things come into being:
> Why not bring them to full development?
> Hence to neglect human effort and think about Heaven
> is to miss the true nature of things (*Ibid.*).

Like Chuang Tzu, Hsün Tzu spoke of a naturalistic Heaven, which contains no ethical principle, but he differed from the Taoist philosopher, inasmuch as he insisted on the independence of man from Heaven and even mastery of Heaven by man rather than the exaltation of Heaven (Nature) at the expense of culture, as advocated by Taoist philosophers.

Since Hsün Tzu proclaimed unequivocally the evil of human nature and the mastery of Heaven by man, it was to be expected that he would place emphasis on knowledge—the knowledge of the sage-kings (ch. XXI). And this knowledge might be acquired, as Hsün Tzu told us, especially by studying the classics as expounded by great teachers. Thus he said:

> Where should learning begin, and where should it end? In point of process, learning begins with reciting the classics, and ends with studying the *li*. In point of purpose, learning begins with cultivation to be a scholar, and ends with cultivation to be a sage (ch. I).

And again:

> Not to consider right the ways of one's teacher, but to prefer one's own ways, is like using a blind man to distinguish colors, or a deaf man to distinguish sounds; *there* is no way to get rid of confusion and error (ch. II).

According to Hsün Tzu, man is not self-sufficient, because he needs learning and the guidance of a teacher. To learn is not just to cultivate one's character, but rather to perform intellectual exercises or simply to acquire external knowledge, which was to be relied upon to suppress or transform the original nature of man. This aspect of Hsün Tzu's philosophy marks another difference between him and Mencius.

In spite of his emphasis on knowledge, Hsün Tzu was not merely an intellectualist. A great thinker, he recognized the importance of desires and emotions and of regulating them by the mind in accordance with *li*. He believed that the means of coping with desires is not to eliminate them; nor is it to diminish them; it is rather to guide them into proper channels. This aspect of Hsün Tsu's philosophy is in complete accord with the idealism of Mencius. Thus Hsün Tzu said:

> Every doctrine of good conduct which depends upon the elimination of desires, has no way of guiding the desires, but is hampered by the presence of desire. Every doctrine of good conduct which expects the lessening of desires has no way to curb the desires but is hampered by the great number of desires. . . . Desire does not depend upon whether attainment is possible, whereas its gratification seeks what is possible. That desire does not depend upon whether attainment is possible, is something attributable to Heaven. That gratification seeks what is possible, is something attributable to the mind. Desires which are attributable to Heaven, are regulated by the mind that is in turn attributable to Heaven. . . . If one's desire surpasses what one's action can afford, the mind will restrain it. If what the mind assents to is in accord with principles, although the desires are many, what detriment are they to good conduct? When one's desire is deficient, but one's action is excessive, the mind has caused it. If what the mind assents to deviates from principles, then although the desires be few, how would that restrain misconduct? Hence good conduct and misconduct depend on the assent of the mind, not on the desires of man's nature. . . . Although desires cannot be eliminated, their pursuit can be temperate. Although desires cannot be fully satisfied, one who seeks for them can nearly satisfy them. Although desire cannot be eliminated, if it cannot be obtained by pursuit, one with thought will restrain its

pursuit. If a man who knows the *Tao* is in power, he will come near to satisfying his desires; if he is out of power, he will restrain his pursuit. There is nothing else in the world better than this (ch. XXII).

From this passage it is obvious that man is born with desires and equipped with mind. Desires cannot be completely eliminated or fully satisfied, but Hsün Tzu recognized the necessity of keeping desire under proper restraint and saw that this is the function of the mind. For the work of the mind is not merely to think but to deal with right or wrong in the moral sense. When the mind is motivated by *li* and *yi*, desires are subdued to human purpose. But because the mind is often confused by desires, Hsün Tzu held that mental purification, as characterized by "emptiness, unity and quiescence" (XXI), is a prerequisite for the attainment of truth and goodness. At this point, Hsün Tzu made a suggestion that was to have great influence over a thousand years later on the Neo-Confucian philosophers of the Sung and Ming periods. We shall deal with this in Chapters 7 and 8, but now we move on to Confucianism as practiced in the Ch'in and Han periods of Chinese history.

5

Confucianism of the Ch'in and Han Periods
(221 B.C. – A.D. 220)

Three Important Essays

Before the triumph of Ch'in under the First Emperor (259–210 B.C.), who united the Chinese people for the first time under a strong central government, there was much intellectual freedom and diversity. In fact, they spoke of the "hundred schools of philosophy." We have seen that these various thinkers and teachers rose out of the social and political chaos with systems of thought that could serve as beacons for China's future development. Thereafter, China has never felt poor in so far as her cultural heritage is concerned. However, in the new age that followed, there was need for peace and unity in the political and intellectual spheres. Toward these ends, the First Emperor, at the suggestion of the Grand Councillor Li Ssu, with Legalist severity decreed, in 213 B.C., that all historical records, except those of Ch'in, should be burned; all libraries of poetry, history and philosophy, except those under the custody of the Eruditi, sent to the officials to be destroyed; only books of medicine, divination, agriculture and arboriculture preserved; and students required to study laws under officials. This decree effectively put an end to freedom of thought as it had existed in the previous period; and as a result, Chinese philosophy, more particularly Confucianism, suffered a decline and lost much of its vitality and appeal.

The Han dynasty (205 B.C.–A.D. 220) resurrected the Confucian classics and revived letters, which had been proscribed under the short-lived Ch'in dynasty (255–206 B.C.). The Confucian school, especially, for a time overshadowed first by Legalism and later by Taoism, now began to recover the dominant position it had held in the Chou period. Thus, in the space of less than a century, the struggle for supremacy was finally won and Confucianism was established as the orthodox doctrine of the new state.

Most of the Confucian thinkers and teachers we have considered held or aspired to government offices of some sort, and most were very much interested in the pressing problems presented by the current political and social chaos, and offered plans for peace and unity. The connection between government and philosophy became especially apparent toward the end of the Chou dynasty and was a fact of Chinese life at the beginning of the Han dynasty.

In the *Han Fei Tzu* (attributed to Han Fei, a Legalist philosopher of the third century B.C.) there is a passage about the later Confucianists:

> Since the death of Confucius, there have appeared the schools of Tzu Chang, Tzu Ssu, Yen [Hui], Mencius, Ch'i-tiao, Chung Liang, Sun [Hsün Tzu] and Yo Cheng (ch. 19).

These eight divisions comprised the main Confucian schools of the end of the Chou period. The writings of these men, together with those of the early Han scholars, were compiled by Tai Te (the Elder Tai) into a single work of eighty-five sections, which was reduced by Tai Sheng (the Younger Tai), the nephew of Tai Te, to forty-six sections. This latter compilation comprises what is now known as the *Li Chi* (The *Book of Rites*), representing an "encyclopedia" of Confucian teachings of late Chou, Ch'in, and Han times.

From the age of Confucius (sixth century B.C.) onward, most Chinese philosophers, particularly Confucianists, attempted to work for an ideal world. They thought of men as related in "one world, one family," so that "within the four seas, all men are brothers" (The *Lun Yü* XII–5). The teachings of Confucius, as well as those of Mencius and Hsün Tzu, stressed the importance of education to foster this sentiment of "one family world," so that one would be able to bring one's goodness to the service of mankind. They recognized that man cannot be separated from the world. In their political philosophy they always tended to place the world before the state and ignored national barriers to consider the unity and peace of the world and the welfare of humanity at large. These lofty ideas, especially those of Mencius and Hsün Tzu, were further elaborated in the three important treatises—the *Ta Hsüeh* (The Great Learning), the *Chung Yung* (The Doctrine of the Mean), and the *Li Yün* (The Evolution of Rites). These short treatises were compiled in the *Li Chi*.

The *Ta Hsüeh* and the *Chung Yung*, which have exercised a great influence on later Chinese philosophy, were combined by the great Sung scholar Chu Hsi (A.D. 1130–1200), with the *Lun Yü* and the *Meng Tzu*, to form the *Four Books*, which became the basis of Confucian education. Let us examine them briefly one by one.

The *Ta Hsüeh* (Great Learning)

In the works of Confucius, Mencius, and Hsün Tzu we have seen Confucianism characterized as man-centered and world-centered, preoccupied in seeking to establish a better world. Every political philosophy reflects, to some extent, the political circumstances of its author. These three great philosophers of ancient China lived in an age marked by war and chaos in political and social life. Major challenges to them were, first, how to end the bloody war between the feudal lords, and, second, how to establish an ideal state like the Great Commonwealth (*Ta-tung*), in which mankind could live happily and harmoniously. In preceding chapters we have not said much about their opinions concerning good government and the ideal state. Now let us turn to the *Ta Hsüeh* to explain the Confucian political philosophy.

The *Ta Hsüeh* was traditionally attributed to Tseng Ts'an, one of the chief disciples of Confucius. It was also attributed to Tzu Ssu, grandson of Confucius and a disciple of Tseng Ts'an. Modern scholars are not certain who the author was, knowing only that several passages are definitely of a much later period than Tseng Ts'an. But whoever its author may be, the treatise represents a concise résumé of Confucian ethical and political philosophy. There are at least nine editions of the text and they vary in the arrangement of paragraphs and in the number of sections. For our purposes the ideas and not the textual problems are of interest.

A unique feature of the *Ta Hsüeh* is the logical reasoning it applies to a general thesis which has come to be called "three guiding principles" and "eight ethico-political items." Its opening section reads:

> The way of Great Learning is to manifest illustrious virtue, to love the people, and to abide in the highest good.

This statement has been known as the "three guiding principles." Once again:

> The ancients who wished clearly to manifest illustrious virtue throughout the world would first govern their own states well. Wishing to govern their states well, they would first regulate their families. Wishing to regulate their families, they would first cultivate their own persons. Wishing to cultivate their persons, they would first rectify their minds. Wishing to rectify their minds, they would first be sincere in their thoughts. Wishing to be sincere in their thoughts, they would first extend their knowledge.

Such extension of knowledge lay in the investigation of things. And conversely, the passage continues:

> Things being investigated, their knowledge became complete. Their knowledge being complete, their thoughts became sincere. Their thoughts being sincere, their minds were rectified. Their minds being rectified, their persons were cultivated. Their persons being cultivated, their families were regulated. Their families being regulated, their states were well governed. Their states being well governed, the world was at peace.

This statement has been known as the "eight ethico-political items," but basic to all, of course, is the cultivation of one's own self. The same passage concludes:

> From the Son of Heaven [the Emperor] down to the common people, all must consider the cultivation of one's own self as the root. It cannot be, when the root is in disorder, that the branches are in order. It has never been, when what is treated with great importance becomes a matter of slight importance, that what is treated with slight importance becomes a matter of great importance. This is called knowing the root; this is also called the perfection of knowledge.

Here is the essence of Confucian ethico-political philosophy. The central thesis is the moral cultivation of one's own self. To be cultivated, according to the *Ta Hsüeh*, would lead to a profound understanding of oneself in relation to others and in relation to the whole world. For its author, self-cultivation is a process of self-realization and self-fulfillment which presupposes self-knowledge and a reference to universal truth, or the *Tao*. The items preceding the self-cultivation—investigation of things, extension of knowledge, sincerity in one's thoughts, and rectification of one's mind—are the ways and means for cultivating and perfecting goodness in one's self, while the items following self-cultivation—a well-ordered family, a well-governed state and a happy and harmonious world—are the ways and means for extending and bringing one's goodness for the service of mankind. This is true to Confucian tradition, stressing moral cultivation as the controlling element in government. Hsün Tzu said: "I have heard of cultivation of the person, but never of conducting affairs of state" (*Hsün Tzu*, ch. VIII). According to Confucian teachings, the order that was to emerge out of chaos was to be grounded on personal moral cultivation.

In the above passages, we note that ethics and politics are inextricably intertwined, which is also characteristic of Confucianism. The author of the *Ta Hsüeh* was thinking of the ideal state in terms of world politics and world peace. In fact, he was not the first to think in this way. For instance, Mencius said:

> People have a common saying: "World, state, family." The root of the world is in the state. The root of the state is in the family. The root of the family is in the individual (*Meng Tzu* IV-A, 5).

The ideas developed in the *Ta Hsüeh* represent a synthesis of Chinese political philosophy and a program of practical politics, leading from the cultivation of one's personal life, through the regulation of one's family and ordering of one's state, to the accomplishment of world peace and harmony for the welfare of humanity at large. Being an all-inclusive and self-consistent program, the book tells us not only how to cultivate ourselves but also how to extend and develop our goodness to cover others, so that our goodness can be perfected and consummated. However, for its author, the good order of one's own state is not the final goal. The highest ideal of a state is "to manifest illustrious virtue throughout the world"; that is, to achieve peace and harmony in the world—the Great Commonwealth, which is the subject of the section of the *Li Chi* entitled *Li Yün* (Evolution of Rites).

Most of the ideas, largely following those of Hsün Tzu, are

elaborated in the second part of the book. But the two important items, "extension of knowledge" (*chih chih*) and "investigation of things" (*ko wu*) which are not clearly explained in the text, have given rise to the most significant controversy between two divergent schools of Neo-Confucianism of the Sung and Ming periods, led by Ch'eng I (1033–1107) and Chu Hsi on the one hand, and by Lu Chiu-yüan (1139–1192) and Wang Yang-ming (1473–1529) on the other hand. The controversy is focused on the question whether *ko wu* should be interpreted as "to investigate things" or "to rectify the mind"; that is, the choice is between objective study and intuitive knowledge. We shall go into the question when we take up Neo-Confucianism in Chapter 8. Now we must move on to the *Chung Yung* (or Doctrine of the Mean), another book incorporated into the collection known as the *Li Chi*.

The *Chung Yung* (Doctrine of the Mean)

The *Chung Yung*, like the *Ta Hsüeh*, was originally included in the *Li Chi*, but was singled out from it by the Sung scholars to form one of the Four Books of Confucianism. Both the *Ta Hsüeh* and the *Chung Yung* were thus elevated to the status of Confucian Classics and exerted a great influence on Chinese thought. The two treatises are quite different. The *Ta Hsüeh* is a treatise primarily dealing with social and political principles, and, true to Confucian tradition, places its emphasis on moral values. On the other hand, the *Chung Yung* is a discourse on metaphysics and concerns the transcendent, although the work accepts the Confucian tradition and has a concern for human affairs. The difference might be summarized as that of the *Tao* of man and the *Tao* of Heaven. Because it represents the *Tao* of man, the *Ta Hsüeh* is concerned with human affairs; because it represents the *Tao* of Heaven, the *Chung Yung* deals with questions that enter into ontological subtleties of metaphysics.

As to its authorship, there is strong and commonly accepted

evidence that the *Chung Yung* was the work of K'ung Chi (or Tzu Ssu), the grandson of Confucius. The *Shih Chi* of Ssu-ma Chien, in the biography of Confucius, states that "Tzu Ssu composed the *Chung Yung*." However, there is some suspicion that some of its passages on philosophical concepts such as *ming* (fate), *hsing* (human nature), *ch'eng* (reality), and *ming* (enlightenment), which seem to be developed from Mencius' doctrines, might be interpolations by followers of Tzu Ssu. These ideas appear to have been influenced by Taoism in the Ch'in or Han period.

Like the *Ta Hsüeh*, the *Chung Yung* begins with the general theme. Clearly stated in the opening section, it reads:

> That which Heaven confers is to be called man's nature. The following of this nature is to be called the *Tao*. The cultivation of the *Tao* is to be called culture [or education].

This short passage stresses the "following of the nature" on the one hand and advocates the "cultivation" of the nature on the other. This leads to a systematic exposition of the "mean" (*chung*) and "normality" (*yung*), which gives the work its title. To secure the mean and normality (*chung yung*) is not merely to pursue a middle course; it means rather to be in harmony with the universe. Thus the way of *chung yung* involves a sense of justice and fairness, a spirit of tolerance, a state of harmony, and a doctrine of equality. It is a way of action which avoids going to extremes. It desires neither too much nor too little. It is also a state of mind in which human reasoning and feeling reach a perfect harmony. In other words, the doctrine of *chung yung*, like the Aristotelian idea of the "golden mean," serves as a guide for human emotions and actions. In the *Chung Yung* we read:

> To have no emotions of pleasure and anger, sorrow and joy, surging up, is to be called being in a state of equilibrium [or mean, *chung*]. To have these emotions surging up, but all in due time, is to be called being in a state of harmony [*ho*].

This state of equilibrium [*chung*] is the supreme foundation of the world, and this state of harmony, its universal path. Once equilibrium and harmony are achieved, Heaven and Earth maintain their proper positions, and the myriad things are nourished.

Equilibrium and harmony, as noted in this short passage, are the keynotes in the *Chung Yung*. As natural feelings of the heart, such emotions as pleasure, anger, sorrow and joy must be allowed expression, but at the same time such feelings must be kept in the mean state, so as to achieve harmony. For harmony results from *chung* (equilibrium or mean), and *chung* serves to harmonize what is discordant. Moreover, this state of harmony must exist not merely in man's mind, but also in his personal conduct and in his social relations. Hence in the *Chung Yung* we read:

> All things are to be nourished and not to injure one another, and all the courses [of the seasons, etc.] are to be pursued and not to collide with one another. The small forces evolve like river currents; the great forces manifest in mighty transformation. It is because of this that Heaven and Earth are great.

This is also a state of harmony on the scale of Heaven and Earth.

In this treatise there is another important concept, *ch'eng* (reality or sincerity), on which it discourses elaborately. *Ch'eng* (or reality) is not just a state of mind; it is rather a motivating force that is transforming things and perfecting things. In its nature there is no distinction between what is within and without, what is of self and of others. Thus it is said in the *Chung Yung*:

> Reality (*ch'eng*) is the Way (*Tao*) of Heaven; making oneself real is the Way of man. To be real is to hit the mean without effort, to possess it without the process of thought, and to be centered in the Way with a natural ease—this is to be a sage. To be real is to choose the good and hold fast to it.

And the *Chung Yung* continues:

> Enlightenment (*ming*) that comes out of reality (*ch'eng*) is to be due to man's nature (*hsing*). Reality that comes out of enlightenment is due to culture [or education]. Given reality, there will be enlightenment; given enlightenment, there will be reality.

As reality is the Way of Heaven, man must resort to the aid of culture, in order, through self-enlightenment, to attain it. Hence the attainment of reality is the Way of man. So it says:

> Reality is self-perfecting, and the way of it is self-directing. Reality is the beginning and end of things; without reality, nothing can come into being. Therefore the Superior Man values reality. For reality does not consist simply in perfecting one's self. It is that whereby one perfects all other things. The perfection of one's self means human-heartedness (*jen*); the perfection of other things means wisdom. Herein lies the character of man's nature. This is the Way whereby the inward and the outward are united. Hence whatever pursues is right and proper.

In this passage we note that perfection of oneself and of other things is the way in which the inward and the outward are united. This is indeed the Confucian ideal state of the world. It is not merely a state of nature, nor is it merely a state of culture. It is the full development of nature through the aid of culture. As noted above, reality is the "quality of nature." But the function of culture is not to put the good into this nature, but to bring nature to its full development. On this point, the *Chung Yung* says:

> Only one who possesses absolute reality can fully develop one's nature. Being able to develop one's nature fully, one can then fully develop the nature of others. Being able to develop the nature of others fully, one can then fully develop

the nature of things. Being able to develop the nature of things fully, one can then assist the transforming and nourishing process of Heaven and Earth. Being able to assist the transforming and nourishing process of Heaven and Earth, one can then form a triad with Heaven and Earth.

Here it is obvious that all men share a universal destiny that is only to be guided by cultivation and perfection of goodness not only in oneself, but in everyone else, to whom an individual is inevitably bound and related. This is true to Confucian tradition: for self-cultivation one must practice *chung* and *shu;* that is, one must do one's best for the sake of others. According to the *Chung Yung,* to perfect oneself is to develop fully what Heaven confers. And to extend one's goodness to others is "to assist the transforming and nourishing process of Heaven and Earth." By so doing, one is able to form a triad with Heaven and Earth. This is what the *Chung Yung* calls "enlightenment" (*ming*); that is, a state of mind in which the individual becomes one with the universe.

In one sense, *ch'eng* (reality) means "perfect virtue," corresponding to Confucius' *jen,* the *summum bonum* of all virtues. But at the same time, *ch'eng* is the Way of Heaven, which transcends and develops man's nature. Hence the *Chung Yung* says:

> It is only the man possessed of supreme realness (*ch'eng*) who can make the warp and woof of the great fabric of human society, who can establish the great foundation of the world, and who can understand the transforming and nourishing process of Heaven and Earth. Can there be anything else beyond himself on which he relies? How pervading is his humanity(*jen*)! How unfathomable is his depth! How overwhelming is his heavenliness! Who can comprehend this if he does not possess superior intelligence and sagely wisdom, if he does not reach out to the spiritual power of Heaven?

The significance of this book as a philosophical work lies in its emphasis on the concept of *ch'eng* or "human realness in action" with its capacity to transform and bring man's nature to its full fruition. This realness to oneself also transcends the distinction between the inward and the outward, and reaches for a confrontation and communion with the ultimate creative source of life and the universe. Even more important, this human realness is to be the controlling element in human relations in general and in government in particular. The *Chung Yung* says:

> The universal Way of the world is five fold, and [the supreme virtue] by which the Way is practiced is threefold. There are the relations of ruler and subject, father and son, husband and wife, elder and younger brother, and between friends; these five [relations] constitute the universal Way of the world. Wisdom (*chih*), humanity (*jen*), and courage (*yung*): these three are the supreme virtues of the world. [The Way] whereby they are practiced is one.

These ideas are evidently close to those of Confucius, making the five relations the universal Way of the world, while the three supreme virtues are the results of *ch'eng* (reality); that is, the one. On the basis of the universal Way, and by means of the three supreme virtues, one may both cultivate one's self and govern others. With regards to government, the *Chung Yung* discourses brilliantly on the duties of the sovereign, as summarized in the following passage:

> There are nine basic duties by which to govern the world and [its contituent] states and families:
> [1] to cultivate one's own person,
> [2] to honor men of worth,
> [3] to be affectionate to one's kinsmen,
> [4] to respect great ministers,
> [5] to be considerate to all officials,
> [6] to treat the common people as children,
> [7] to promote the hundred crafts,
> [8] to be hospitable to strangers,
> [9] to be friendly to the feudal princes.

Here again the way whereby these basic duties are carried out is "one"; that is, *ch'eng*. It is obvious that, true to the great tradition of the Confucian school, the author of the book stressed that good government depended upon good administration, thus underscoring the need of moral cultivation on the part of the ruling class.

The *Li Yün* (Evolution of Rites)

We have said that for Confucius and his followers the good order of one's own state was not the final goal. The ideal which they held highest was the Great Commonwealth, which they called *Ta T'ung*. Confucius himself did not give us a picture of this ideal. It was formulated for us in a short treatise on the *Li Yün*, attributed to the Sage and compiled in the *Li Chi*. This work, which was borrowed or at least was influenced by the social and political ideas of the rival schools, especially of Taoism, assumed the greatest importance in the Han dynasty.

In mapping out this grand scheme for the coming of the new era, the author of the *Li Yün* divided the progress of the world into two important epochs—the era of Small Tranquility (*Hsiao K'ang*) and the era of Great Commonwealth (*Ta T'ung*). Its author put the Great Commonwealth into the golden ages of antiquity, when sage-kings like Yao, Shun, Yu, and Tang resigned. As a matter of fact, it was merely a world Utopia of the Han scholar, who attempted to provide this theory of *Ta T'ung* with an institutional justification of the ancient sage-kings. Nevertheless, his ideal world is a beautiful vision and yet a more tangible one than all the Republics and Utopias put together.

Of the Great Commonwealth, the *Li Yün* says:

> When the great *Tao* prevailed, the world was common to all. Men of talent and virtue were selected; mutual confidence was emphasized and brotherhood was cultivated. Therefore,

men did not regard as parents only their own parents, nor did they treat as sons only their own sons. A competent provision was secured for the aged till their death; employment [was provided] for the able-bodied; the means of growing up [was provided] for the young. Kindness and compassion were shown to widows, orphans, childless men, and cripples, so that they were all well cared for. Men had their respective occupations, and women their homes. They hated to see the wealth lying about in waste, and yet they did not hoard it for their own use. They hated not to use their energies, and yet they used their energies not for their own benefit. In this way, selfish schemes were repressed and could not develop. Robbers, thieves, and rebellious traitors did not arise, and hence the front doors remained open. This was the era of what is called the Great Commonwealth.

Here is the essence of the *Ta-t'ung* doctrine, envisioning a practicable Utopia realized through the idea of democracy, social security, communized wealth, and also world government, shared by all the people, who create it and benefit from it. These utopian and socialist ideas are evidently appropriated from the social and political philosophy of the Taoists and Mo Tzu. Such syncretic and eclectic tendencies characterized the Han period in the field of philosophy, when old materials and new were used to build edifices of thought and philosophers borrowed and adapted as well as created.

Though the author of the *Li Yün* spoke of the era of the Great Commonwealth as a golden age at the dawn of history, he certainly saw it as a vision of the future, following the era of Small Tranquility. Hence the same passage continues:

Now the great *Tao* has fallen into obscurity, and the world has been in the possession of families. Each regards as parents only his own parents, and treats as sons only his own sons. Wealth and labor are employed for selfish purposes. The sovereigns take it as the proper *li* that their states should be hereditary; they endeavor to make their cities and suburbs strong, their ditches and moats secure. *Li* and *yi* are used as the norms to regulate the relationship between ruler and subject, to insure affection between father and son, harmony between brothers, and concord between husband and wife; to set up institutions, organize farms and hamlets, honor the brave and the wise, and bring the merit to one's own self. Hence intrigue and plotting come about and men thereby take up arms.

It was in this way Yü, T'ang, Wen, Wu [founders of the Hsia, Shang, and Chou dynasties], King Cheng and Duke Chou achieved eminence. All these six rulers paid attention to *li*. Thus they made manifest their righteousness (*yi*) and acted in good faith; they exposed their errors, abided by *jen*, practiced prudence, thus showing the people what they should constantly comply with. If there were any who did not follow these principles, he would lose power and position and be regarded by the multitude as dangerous. This was the era of what is called the Small Tranquility (*Hsiao K'ang*).

In the passage, it is obvious that the author of the *Li Yün* was dissatisfied with the government and society of the Small Tranquility, though it had been the care of Confucius and Mencius to establish the government of that period along the best and most just lines. The doctrine of *Ta T'ung* exemplified here represents an advance over the political philosophy of Confucius, Mencius, and Hsün Tzu, as the ideal period it refers to is superior to the period in which they lived. In more recent times this lofty ideal was advocated by K'ang Yu-wei (1858–1927) and Sun Yat-sen (1866–1925), although they differed in their interpretation of what the ideal government ought to be, both in goals and in structure. In time we shall come to a consideration of twentieth-century Chinese thought and discuss the influence of Confucianism upon things of our own age, but now we must pass to something very important in the development of Confucianism, the amalgamation of the *Yin-Yang* and Confucian schools.

6

The Yin-Yang *School of Confucianism: Tung Chung-shu*

The Triumph of Confucianism

As far as we know, Confucianism became the predominant philosophy in China only after the imperial system was consolidated under the Ch'in and Han dynasties. There was a good reason for this. Since the time of Confucius himself, the feudal lords had been so preoccupied with conquest and defense, so embroiled in internecine struggles, that they had no time for doctrines and ideology. However, when China was unified and became the Empire, the sovereigns began to look for ways and means of ensuring political stability and ideological control by rooting out the thoughts and sentiments that might endanger the regime they had established. As we have noted above, the First Emperor of Ch'in, absolutely a Legalist monarch, took drastic measures to eradicate dangerous doctrines by burning books and burying scholars alive. The Han rulers took a different approach to the problem of thought control. Though they disapproved of the drastic methods of the Ch'in, they also realized that it was wise to unify the thought of the empire in order to maintain political unity. It is commonly said that this new attempt was made during the reign of Wu Ti (140–87

B.C.), who selected Confucianism and gave it preëminence as the state orthodoxy. This innovation was in fact the work of Tung Chung-shu (179?–104? B.C.), the greatest of the early Han scholars. In a memorial presented to the emperor, he advocated a system of education based squarely on Confucianism. Thus it was he who created the institutional basis for Confucian orthodoxy, the famed Chinese examination system. However, it should be noted that Confucianism as propounded by Tung Chung-shu and adopted in the early Han period, developed into something very different from the early Confucianism of the Chou period. Tung Chung-shu worked out a new philosophical interpretation and justification for the Han imperial institution, and the result was one of the great achievements of Chinese thought.

Han Confucianism gained supremacy not by extinguishing its rival schools but by adapting many of their ideas, especially those of Taoism, and incorporating them into its own system. None of the pre-Ch'in schools of thought survived into Han times as distinct philosophical systems. Even Legalism, which helped to unify the imperial rule by strict regulation and autocratic power, had fallen into disgrace, but its political theory still lingered in the mind of the ruling class. Taoism, the chief rival of Confucianism, had in the early Han period become very influential among government officials; they adopted the Taoist doctrine of *wu wei* (inaction) as their state policy and its occultism as their personal creed. This fact determined the general character of Han Confucianism.

Generally speaking, the Han scholars divided themselves into two groups; one known as the New Script school (so-called because its version of the Confucian classics was written in the current script) and the other as the Old Script school (so-called because it claimed to possess the ancient texts which existed before the time when "the Ch'in fire" burned the books). The controversy between these two schools was one of the most bitter in the history of Chinese scholarship. Their disagreement on the texts of the Confucian classics was exacerbated by a difference in their views about Confucius and Confucianism. The New Script school considered Confucius a "throneless king" and a savior of the world, as claimed in the apocryphal literature. In opposition to this view, the Old Script school maintained that Confucius was essentially a sage and inherited the cultural legacy of the past, to which he gave new interpretations and which he transmitted to posterity. We also find the scholars of the New Script school expounding the Confucian classics in terms of *yin-yang* doctrine.[1] Indeed with *yin* and *yang* they developed a vast and intricate system for the analysis and control of natural phenomena. In spite of its absurdities, the New Script school, under the leadership of Tung Chung-shu became popular in the Han period. The increased interest in Confucianism even led to an increase in the number of texts. All the circumstances of the time encouraged forgery of Confucian books. Pecuniary rewards, imperial favor and popular esteem, even the desire on the part of scholars to lend the authority of the Master of their own ideas, all encouraged zealous scholars to exercise their inventive faculties in the production of plausible substitutes for the lost books. The kind of Confucianism developed under the influence of the New Script school was a great synthesis of a variety of philosophies and superstitions, but every aspect of it at least pretended to be derived from Confucius and his great tradition.

Tung Chung-shu's Life and His Position in Confucianism

That many scholars fixed upon the reign of Wu Ti as the period of triumph of Confucianism should not surprise us. One of Wu Ti's first acts, under the influence of Confucian scholars, was to expel all students of Legalism from court and to reorganize the Board of Eruditi into five faculties, each specializing in one of the five Confucian classics: the *Shu Ching* (Book of History), the *Shih Ching* (Book of Poetry), the *I Ching* (Book of Change), the *Li Chi*, and the *Ch'un Ch'iu* (Spring and Autumn). Later (in 124 B.C.) another innovation was introduced at the suggestion of the Confucian scholars at court. This was the creation of a sort of imperial university, to which fifty students were admitted to study under the Eruditi. It was from this modest beginning that the university quickly grew to 3000 students in the second half of the first century B.C. and to 30,000 students in the second century A.D. At the same time many other schools were founded in the outlying districts more or less on the model of that in the capital for the purpose of training young men in the knowledge of the Confucian classics.

An even more important measure in promoting Confucian doctrine was the introduction of an examination system based on the Five Classics. By 1 A.D. a hundred men a year were said to enter government service through what we would call civil service examinations. Thus from Wu Ti's time on, a large proportion of officials was recruited through a Confucian education at government expense. In this way, the Confucian scholars secured a firm grip on the country's bureaucracy and at the same time also firmly established their hold on China's intellectual life. Not much is known of the life of Tung Chung-shu to whom so much of this can be said to be owed. The *Ch'ien Han Shu* (History of the Former Han Dynasty) (ch. 56) says of him:

> Tung Chung-shu was a native of Kuang-ch'uan (in the southern part of Hopei). In his early years, he studied the *Ch'un Ch'iu* and during the reign of Hsiao-ching (156–141 B.C.) he became an erudite. He gave his lectures behind a curtain, and his teachings were transmitted by his disciples, from one to another, to a remote distance, so that there were some who never saw his countenance. He was so devoted [to his studies] that for three years he did not even take a look at his garden. In his conduct and manner, there is nothing that did not conform to propriety. Scholars all regarded him as a teacher to be respected. . . .
>
> (Tung) Chung-shu's writings all served to elucidate the meaning of the classics. His memorials to the emperor, together with his own instructions, totaled 123 sections. More-

over, his exposition of the success and failure [as recorded] in the *Ch'un Ch'iu*, including "Exaltation of Tradition," "Jade Goblet," "Luxuriant Dew," "Pure Brightness," and "Bamboo Grove," came to several additional tens of sections, amounting to more than 100,000 words. These were all transmitted to later generations.

Here we can see Tung Chung-shu's eminent position among the Confucian scholars of the early Han period. He was renowned for his ability to interpret omens and portents and for his analysis of the *Ch'un Ch'iu* as a book which, he believed, embodies the authentic teachings of Confucius on the philosophy of government. Thus the *Ch'ien Han Shu* (ch. 27) says "In the days of [Emperors] Ching and Wu, Tung Chung-shu studied the *Kung-yang Ch'un Ch'iu*[2] and began to put forward the *yin-yang* [doctrine]. He became the greatest Confucian scholar [of his time]." An examination of his writings will reveal that his teaching was a philosophical synthesis, largely Confucian in inspiration but containing much borrowed from supernatural ideas of the *yin-yang* school. His work, *Ch'un Ch'iu fan-lu* (*Luxuriant Dew of the Spring and Autumn Annals*), consisting of a series of short essays on problems of cosmology and political philosophy, is a rather far-fetched interpretation of the *Ch'un Ch'iu*, in accordance with the prevalent doctrines of the *Kung-yang* school. In the interpretation of these doctrines he made an ingenious discovery of a formula —"to subject the people to the ruler, and the ruler to Heaven" —that acted wonderfully as a check on the absolute sway of the monarch. We shall see his cleverness as we examine his thought in the following section.

Tung Chung-shu's Philosophy

As early as the time of Mencius, there was already a tendency among Confucian scholars to take an interest in the supernatural. This prompted a strong protest from Hsün Tzu, who insisted in his essay "On Heaven" (XVII) that the pursuit of knowledge be restricted to human affairs. Nonetheless in Han times members of the New Script school showed a strong inclination toward cosmic speculation and were not at all content to be as down to earth as Hsün Tzu had been. Tung Chung-shu's "Science of Catastrophes and Anomalies" was in line with the superstitious beliefs of his time and in Section 30 of *Ch'un Ch'iu fan-lu* we read:

> According to a rough classification, when the creatures of Heaven and Earth display unusual changes, these are called "anomalies;" lesser ones are called "catastrophes." The catastrophes always appear first and are then followed by anomalies. Catastrophes are the warnings of Heaven; anomalies are its threats. Heaven first sends warnings, and if [man, being thus warned,] fails to understand, then he is made to feel awe through such anomalies. This is what is meant in the *Shih* when it says: "Stand in awe of the swaying power of Heaven." The genesis of all such catastrophes and anomalies is the direct result of errors that exist within the nation. When the first indications of errors begin to appear in the nation, Heaven sends forth fearful catastrophes to warn men. If, being thus warned, [men] fails to understand [the reason for] these manifestations, then ominous anomalies appear to terrify him. And if, being thus terrified, he still does not understand [the cause for] his fear, only then do misfortunes and calamities visit him. From this we may see that Heaven's will is benevolent, for it has no desire to bring ruin upon man.

The central idea of Tung Chung-shu's system may be summarized as follows: Because of the correspondence of man and Nature and the great similarity in the social and cosmic orders, human actions affect the universal course of Heaven and Earth and manifest themselves in the natural phenomena. Man's wicked deeds, for instance, lead to catastrophes such as fires, floods, droughts, and earthquakes, and anomalies such as comets, eclipses, and weird animals. As Tung Chung-shu writes:

"All things depart from that which is different from themselves and follow that which is similar to themselves. . . .
There is nothing supernatural in this. It is because of their
numerical [harmonies]. [Likewise] fair deeds summon all
things of fair nature, and evil deeds summon all things of evil
nature, just as like answers like" (Sec. 57).

Applying this theory of correspondence of Nature to man,
he further writes:

"When an emperor or a king is about to arise, auspicious
omens first appear, whereas when he is about to be destroyed,
evil auguries likewise first appear. Thus it is that things of the
same kind call to one another" (*Ibid.*).

According to Tung Chung-shu, Heaven can always influence
man through such portents as comets and eclipses, because both
of them are governed by the cosmic forces of *yin* (negative
principle) and *yang* (positive principle). Thus he writes:

Heaven possesses the *yin* and *yang*, and man also possesses
the *yin* and *yang*. When the universe's cosmic force of *yin*
arises, man's cosmic force of *yin* arises in response. And conversely, when man's cosmic force of *yin* arises, the universe's
cosmic force of *yin* should also arise in response. The principle is the same. He who understands this, when he wishes to
bring rain, will activate the *yin* [in man] in order to arouse the
yin [of the universe]; when he wishes to stop rain, he will activate the *yang* [in man] in order to arouse the *yang* [of the
universe]. Therefore the bringing of rain is nothing supernatural. . . . It is not only the cosmic forces of the *yin* and
yang that can approach or withdraw according to their kind.
Even the way whereby misfortunes, calamities, and blessings
are produced follows the same principle. It is nothing but a
case in which one starts something oneself and things act in
response according to their kind (*ibid.*).

In his belief in the correspondence between natural phenomena and human actions, Tung Chung-shu insisted that

"when the world is well governed and the people are at peace,
. . . then the transforming influences of Heaven and Earth
operate in a state of perfection"; conversely, "when the world
is in disorder and the people become perverse, . . . then the
transforming influences of Heaven and Earth suffer injury, so
that the cosmic forces [of the *yin* and *yang*] will cause calamities and harms to arise" (Sec. 81).

Tung Chung-shu made great use of the *yin-yang* theory in
formulating a new ethical and political philosophy of his own.
For instance, he applied the *yin-yang* theory as a metaphysical
justification of the social order. Thus he writes:

> In all things there must be correlates. Thus there are such
> correlates as upper and lower, left and right, external and in-
> ternal, beauty and ugliness, obedience and disobedience, and
> joy and anger, cold and heat, day and night. These are all cor-
> relates. The *yin* is the correlate of the *yang*, the wife of hus-
> band, the son of the father, the people of the sovereign. There
> is nothing that does not have such correlates, and in each cor-
> relation there is the *yin* and *yang*. Thus the relationships be-
> tween sovereign and people, father and son, husband and wife,
> are all derived from the principles of the *yin* and *yang*. The
> sovereign is *yang*, the people are *yin;* the father is *yang*, the
> son *yin;* the husband is *yang*, the wife *yin*. . . . The "three
> bonds" [*san kang*], comprising the "kingly way" [*wang tao*],
> may be sought in Heaven (Sec. 53).

Of the "five cardinal human relationships" three—those of
sovereign and people, father and son, husband and wife—are
singled out as the "three bonds," according to which the sovereign, father, and husband are the "bonds" of the people, son,
and wife. Tung Chung-shu, by subjecting "people to sovereign, son to father, and wife to husband," made the doctrine of
the "three bonds" a ready tool for autocracy to maintain social
order. He also attempted to provide a metaphysical justification
for the existing social relationships by saying that these relationships "are all derived from the principles of the *yin* and *yang*."

If we take this doctrine in its social and political context we shall see that its esteem for the superior over the inferior contributed to the growing authoritarianism of the imperial government.

At the same time Tung Chung-shu's system of Confucianism contained ideas and concepts that acted as a check on the absolute sway of the monarch. The doctrine of the "three bonds" is underscored by the concept of *yüan* (or origin). The meaning of *yüan* is explained in the following passage:

> What is called the single *yüan* is the great beginning. . . . It is only the sage who can relate the myriad things to the One and thus link them to *yüan*. If the source is not traced and the development from it followed, nothing can be accomplished. . . . This *yüan* is the same as a source. It means that *yüan* permeates Heaven and Earth from beginning to end. . . . Therefore *yüan* is the root of all things, and in it lies man's origin (Sec. 13).

Here we find that the concept of *yüan* is not much different from that of *T'ai Chi* (the Supreme Ultimate) in the *I Ching* (*Book of Changes*). But the concept of *T'ai Chi* is confined to the field of metaphysics, whereas the concept of *yüan* is applied to social and political affairs. According to Tung Chung-shu, for all things in the universe there is something from which they derive their being. He calls it "the root of all things." In discussing its abstract principle, the "root" is called *Yüan;* in speaking of its actual application, it is called "Heaven and Earth." Hence it is said: "Put together, the cosmic forces of Heaven and Earth constitute a unity" (Sec. 58). Since Earth is "the assister of Heaven" (Sec. 42), it is evident that Heaven is the primary "root of all things."

Then Tung Chung-shu further asserts:

> What produces [man] cannot [itself] be man, for the creator of man is Heaven. The fact that man is man derives from Heaven. Heaven, indeed, is man's great ancestor. This is why man is to be classed with Heaven above. Man's physical body is given form through the transforming influence of Heaven's

numerical [laws]. Man's vital force is directed to humanity (*jen*) through the transforming influence of Heaven's will. Man's virtuous conduct is expressed in righteousness (*yi*) through the transforming influence of Heaven's principle. . . . The duplicate of Heaven lies in man, and man's feelings and nature derive from Heaven (Sec. 41).

Here we can see the intimate relationship of Heaven and man. Since "man receives his life from" and "is classed with Heaven above," it follows that he should study and comprehend the laws of Heaven—Heaven in both a divine and a physical sense. Hence Tung Chung-shu says: "The great source of basic principles (*tao*) derives from Heaven" (*Ch'ien Han Shu*, ch. 56). But "Heaven holds its position on high" and so is beyond the reach of the people. This is why they require a king to instruct them: he acts as a link between Heaven and man. "It is only the emperor," Tung Chung-shu asserts, "who receives the Decree of Heaven, and the world which receives the edict of the Emperor" (Sec. 41). Likewise, in Tung's opinion, the principal object of the *Ch'un Ch'iu* was "to subject the people to the ruler, and the ruler to Heaven" (Sec. 23). This ingenious idea acted wonderfully as a useful weapon with which to combat misgovernment on the part of the monarch; for even though the emperor's powers were unlimited, he was at least subject to the judgments of Heaven as manifested in the abnormalities of nature. Heaven could communicate to his subjects his displeasure with an emperor. That this was in some measure successful is attested by the imperial edicts recorded in the *Ch'ien Han Shu*, in which the emperor requested the ministers and people to remonstrate with him on his misdeeds whenever anything of ill omen occurred. Absolute as he was, the emperor could be called to task.

The king, being thus entrusted by Heaven with the task of ruling men, holds a supreme position and heavy responsibility to humanity. Thus Tung Chung-shu writes:

The ancients, when they invented writing, drew three lines and connected them through the middle, calling this "king"

[王]. The three lines are Heaven, Earth, and man, and that which passes the middle joins the principles of all three. Occupying the center of Heaven, Earth, and man, so as to pass through and join all three—who, if not a king, could do this? (Sec. 43).

Man, Heaven, and Earth form an inseparable triad. It is to be expected that the emperor, the head of men, is responsible for keeping mankind in harmony with Heaven and Earth. Such is the argument of Tung Chung-shu:

> The ruler is the basis [or root] of the state. In administering the state, nothing is more effective for instructing the people than reverence for the basis. . . . What do we mean by the basis? Heaven, Earth, and man are the basis of all creatures. Heaven produces them, Earth nourishes them, and man completes them. Heaven provides them at birth with filial piety and fraternal love; Earth nourishes them with clothing and food; man completes them with rites and music. These three are to each other like the hands and feet, which join to complete the physical form, so that none can be dispensed with. . . . Hence the enlightened and worthy ruler, being of good faith, is strictly attentive to the three bases. His sacrifices are conducted with utmost reverence; he makes offerings to and serves his ancestors; he advances fraternal love and encourages filial conduct. In this way he serves the basis of Heaven. He personally grasps the plow handle and plows a furrow, plucks the mulberry himself and feeds the silkworms, breaks new ground to increase the grain supply, and opens the way for a sufficiency of clothing and food. In this way he serves the basis of Earth. He sets up schools for the nobles and in the towns and villages to teach filial piety and fraternal love, reverence and humility. He enlightens the people with education and moves them with rites and music. Thus he serves the basis of man. If he rightly serves these three [bases], then the people will be like sons and brothers, not daring to be unsubmissive (Sec. 19).

Here we can see that man's task is to make a perfect completion of what Heaven and Earth have left incomplete. This is how man is able to form a triad with Heaven and Earth; that is, "the basis of all creatures." Hence "the enlightened and worthy ruler is strictly attentive to the three bases." These are performance of sacrifices, economic well-being and moral education of the people. To all these, as to Tung's advocacy of a hierarchy of mankind, Confucianists agreed. In this connection, the following passage from the *Hsün Tzu* is worth quoting:

> Heaven has its seasons, Earth its resources, and man his government. This is how man is able to form a triad with Heaven and Earth. If man neglects his own part in this triad and puts all his hope in Heaven and Earth with which he forms a triad, he is making a grave mistake (ch. 17).

The significance of Tung Chung-shu as a philosopher lies in his ability to coordinate the "seasons of Heaven," the "resources of Earth," and the "government of man" into a single comprehensive "science." His cosmic speculations carried him into metaphysical areas which Confucius refused to delve into and Hsün Tzu openly admonished men not to explore, so along with his sound ideas was a wealth of pseudo-scientific beliefs, which Tung Chung-shu called the "Science of Catastrophe and Anomalies," and which had a tremendous influence upon the Han political thought.

Tung Chung-shu's famous work (the *Ch'un-Ch'iu fan-lu*) was in fact what today we might think of as a very "far out" interpretation of Confucius' *Ch'un Ch'iu* but it struck a responsive chord because it was fully in accordance with the prevalent beliefs of the time. Tung Chung-shu held that Confucius received the Mandate of Heaven to become a king, so that the Sage wrote the *Ch'un Ch'iu* entrusting the kingship to Lu State and establishing institutions for a new dynasty. Tung Chung-shu argued for a doctrine of Three Reigns, according to which there were three institutional patterns (Black, White and Red), each of which rested on a different principle and was suitable for a different regime. A different system of institutions was adopted by a new dynasty to replace that of the defunct one, so as to show that the new dynasty had received the new Mandate from Heaven which cancelled that of its predecessor. This was an exceptionally strange idea, but Tung Chung-shu believed it and justified his system by quotation from it. He further divided the two hundred and forty-two years of history covered by the *Ch'un Ch'iu* (722–481 B.C.) into three periods, which he called the "Three Ages," that is: the age witnessed by Confucius, the age based on the oral testimony, and the age evidenced by transmitted records (Sec. 1). According to Tung Chung-shu, Confucius, when writing the *Ch'un Ch'iu,* used different words or phrases to record events occurring in the three periods. Hence he insisted that in the analysis of its phraseology, one might discover the "esoteric dicta and great dogmas" (*wei-yen ta-i*) of the *Ch'un Ch'iu.*

Later the *Kung-yang* school of the *Ch'un Ch'iu* elaborated the theory of the Three Ages. This group argued that the course of human history is a steady progress from the Age of Disorder through the Age of Approaching Peace, to the Age of Universal Peace. This theory of the Three Ages also appears in the short treatise known as the *Li Yün* (Evolution of Rites), one of the sections in the *Li Chi* that we discussed in Chapter 5.

Tung Chung-shu was deeply religious as well as somewhat superstitious. He had used a religious disposition to glorify the Confucian school and Confucius. According to Tung Chung-shu, Confucius was not only the first to found a particular school of thought, but the Sage was in addition the true king of a particular age. It is hard to say whether in advancing this theory Tung Chung-shu was original or merely reflecting some prevalent beliefs of the Han period. Whatever the case, this idea was accepted by the Han Confucian scholars. The apocryphal literature began to call Confucius the "son of the Black Emperor [*ti*]." The attempt to deify Confucius went on uninterrupted for many centuries in and after the Han dynasty. As early as A.D. 56, a beginning was made in the Confucian cult when Emperor Ming (A.D. 58–75) of the later Han dynasty ordered sacrifices, hitherto confined to the temple at the burial place of Confucius in Lu, to be made in all the schools in the cities. This clearly established the Sage as the patron saint of education. After that there was an effort to accelerate the canonization of Confucius and it was widely supported by Confucian scholars. Confucius' temples were built in almost every prefectural city throughout the empire. A complete code of sacrificial ritual was drawn up for the worship of Confucius. The Confucian cult was already well-established in the T'ang dynasty (618–907).

CHAPTER 7

The Rise of
Neo-Confucianism

We have seen that after the death of Confucius, Confucianism underwent several stages of intellectual development. The first stage was reached shortly before the Ch'in dynasty, when Mencius and Hsün Tzu established two rival schools of thought and developed Confucius' teaching in two directions. The second stage culminated with Tung Chung-shu and many other scholars of the Kung-yang school in the Han period, when a variety of pseudo-scientific reasoning and cosmological speculations was grafted onto Confucianism. Now we come to a third stage, that of the Neo-Confucianists of the Sung period (960–1279), when the elements of Taoism and Buddhism were appropriated to give Confucianism a philosophical refinement hitherto unknown.

Neo-Confucianism, usually known as *Li-hsüeh* (Philosophy of Principle) or *Hsing-li hsüeh* (Philosophy of Human Nature and Principle), began in the eighth century, flourished vigorously in the eleventh and twelfth centuries, and produced notable interpreters and critics right down to recent times. The word *Neo-Confucianism* is in fact a misnomer. It does not mean a genuine revival of Confucianism. The founders of Neo-Confucianism were no doubt Confucian scholars, but their intellectual activity was stimulated and determined by Buddhist and Taoist ideologies. They were able to extend the horizon of the Confucian ethical and political doctrines to include cosmology and metaphysics. Specifically, the Neo-Confucian scholars worked out a new cosmic order to match the Buddhist cosmology and a system of moral philosophy to explain the Confucian ethics in metaphysical terms. No doubt Neo-Confucianism was rooted in Confucian tradition, but it displayed some features which went so far beyond the tradition that they would not have been recognizable to Chou or Han Confucianists, let alone the Master himself. Nevertheless, the Neo-Confucian system, though it diverged in many ways from the teachings of Confucius, was ultimately to be regarded as orthodox Confucianism! As such it dominated Chinese thought down to the nineteenth century.

Introduction of Buddhism

Before we discuss Neo-Confucianism, some consideration must be given to the history of Buddhism in China from the third to the tenth century, because Buddhism played a crucial role in Neo-Confucianism. This was the period when Chinese civilization, long more or less immune to "barbarian" influence, cut off from the rest of the world, began to be infused with the cultures of foreign countries. The philosophical thought of this period might be represented by the Taoist metaphysics of the Wei-Tsin period (220–420), known as the *hsüan hsüeh* (literally, "mysterious learning") and Buddhism of the Sui (581–618) and T'ang (618–907) dynasties, which had little connection with politics, but exercised a great influence on Chinese culture. During this period, Buddhism of Indian origin, in collaboration with Chinese Taoism, flourished in China and overshadowed Confucianism. The Buddhist scriptures, translated into Chinese, grew to vast proportions, and its temples and followers multiplied so rapidly that they had to be checked by imperial decree.

Here it should be noted that there is a difference between the terms "Chinese Buddhism" and "Buddhism in China." To state it briefly, "Buddhism in China" was represented by the School of Subjective Idealism (the *Vijnanavada* school). This was the form of Buddhism that clung to the Indian tradition and played little part in the development of Chinese philosophy. "Chinese Buddhism" was represented by the Middle Path school (*Madhyamika* school). This was the form which has been close to Chinese thought and developed in conjunction with Chinese philosophy. There was some similarity between the Middle Path school of Buddhism and Chinese Taoism, and their interaction with each other resulted in *Ch'an* (*Zen* in Japanese) or the *Dhyana* school.

The Chinese term *ch'an* or *ch'an-na* is derived from the Sanskrit *dhyana*, usually translated as "meditation." Originally, *ch'an* meant "directly pointing to the human mind" and "becoming a Buddha by seeing one's own Buddha-nature" or "by identifying the individual with the Universal Mind." This was to be achieved through meditation. *Ch'anism* is a philosophy of silence through its emphasis on "a special transmission outside of the Sacred Teaching." One looks within one's self, not to books, for the enlightenment. Its meditation doctrine is based not on classic Buddhist scriptures but on enlightenment through "the realization of the individual original identification with the Universal Mind." What is meant by "the Universal Mind" is a question to which the *Ch'an* masters have various answers, but in general it is conceived as "the Void," that is, something that cannot be designated by words or perceived by physical senses. One can sympathize, then, with Ch'an masters who find definition difficult. Their methods, however, were clearer: to penetrate the Universal Mind, *Ch'an* masters recommended either *wu nien* ("absence of thoughts") or *wang ch'ing* ("ignoring our feelings") or they were content to permit *jen hsin* ("letting the mind follow its own course").

Anyone who knows anything of Taoism can see that the teachings of *Ch'an* masters have much in common with Taoism. It was said of Hui-neng (627–713), founder of the *Ch'an* school, that "he did not at all understand Buddhism. He understood *Tao* and no other thing." As a matter of fact, the early Buddhist writers used Taoist terminology, such as *yu* ("being"), *wu* ("nonbeing"), *yu wei* ("action"), and *wu wei* ("inaction") to express Buddhist ideas. Sudden Enlightenment, which leads to Buddhahood, is often referred to by the *Ch'an* masters as the "vision of *Tao*." Thus Buddhism of Indian origin readily appealed to Chinese followers of Taoism. When they synthesized it with Chinese Taoism, it was transformed into a Chinese form of Buddhism. Once again the Chinese had assimilated an "invader" and naturalized him.

The most significant element of *Ch'anism* is the emphasis on mind. The mind must be sharpened and sensitized before it can perceive its identification with the Universal Mind. For this purpose the *Ch'an* masters developed various techniques which are quite different from those of Indian *dhyana*. The result was that Chinese *ch'an* can be distinguished from Indian *dhyana* by at least two major points, which we need mention only briefly. First, whereas Indian *dhyana* is conceived as religious enlightenment and stresses concentration and ability to ignore outside influences, Chinese *ch'an* is regarded as philosophical wit and emphasizes wisdom and the ability to handle critical situations. The Chinese predilection for practical application of everything, even abstruse philosophical ideas and mystical states, is clear here in what they did to transform the arcane Indian mysticism into a useful tool. Second, whereas in Indian *dhyana* the mind tries to ignore external influence and aims at intellectual understanding, in Chinese *ch'an* the mind works with the aid of external influence and aims at self-realization. The Chinese like to see things as a whole, not to compartmentalize. This is another aspect of their utilitarian approach.

It is important to note that in the Sung dynasty (960–1279) Buddhism permeated intellectual life perhaps more deeply and thoroughly than at any other time. This was the age when Buddhist doctrines were tailored to Confucianism and cut to Chinese fashion, and when Neo-Confucianism flourished, partly religious and partly philosophical. In other words, Buddhism acted upon Confucianism and produced a highly characteristic form of Neo-Confucianism, and yet the Indian Buddhism became the Chinese, almost unrecognizable in the end product as originating outside the Middle Kingdom.

The close relationship between Buddhism and Neo-Confucianism may be seen in the following illustrations. The state of *nirvana*, according to Buddhism, is a state of stillness in the mind. But to the Confucianists (being Chinese) for the universe and the human mind the essential state is that of permanent activity. Thus the *I Ching* (*Book of Changes*) declares: "The movement of the heavenly bodies is constant, and the Superior Man seeks to improve himself without rest." In resolving this difference, Neo-Confucianism developed the conception of "stillness which is in constant activity, and activity which is in constant stillness." This conception was applied and extended in the doctrine of mind. There are several analogies that Neo-Confucianists like to make. The mind is like a mirror: all the varied images that fall upon its surface are unceasingly active while the mirror remains still and is not bewildered. The mind is like the sun; the clouds pass and vanish under it, but the sun remains constant and is not reflected. Also, the mind is like the vast surface of the sea: the waves rise and fall over it, but the general level remains calm and is not disturbed. For the mind is not outside the activity; it is in fact the mind which is active; but while it is active it remains still. This union of stillness and activity is the highest and best state of mind.

Moreover, according to Buddhism, the visible world is an illusion, a fiction of the imagination; it is unreal, empty, the Great Void. But according to Confucianism, there is an objective world, co-existing with man's own subjective idea of it. Neo-Confucianism resolves this difficulty by accepting that the external world is an "emptiness," a void, while insisting that it has a kind of illusory substantiality. As Chang Tsai (1020–77), a great philosopher of the Sung period, said: "The immensity of space, though called the Great Void, is not void at all. It is filled with *ch'i* [primordial essence]. In fact there is no such thing as vacuum." *Ch'i* is a concept that has become very important in the cosmological and metaphysical theories of the later Neo-Confucianists.

And again, Buddhism is generally regarded as an other-worldly philosophy, because it holds that life itself is the cause of its own misery, that the present world is but "a sea of bitterness." But Confucianism was very much this-worldly in its outlook and essentially humanistic, occupying itself with human relations and shunning questions of the supernatural. Neo-Confucianism resolves this conflict by attempting a synthesis between the two original schools of thought. In this way, Confucianism has been recast on a more speculative, systematic and metaphysical basis, after its contact with Buddhism. This revitalized Confucianism, commonly referred to as Neo-Confucianism, was to become dominant during the Sung and Ming (1368–1644) dynasties.

The Pioneers of the Neo-Confucian Movement

The political chaos of the Six Dynasties (220–580), which was considered as the Dark Ages of China, had contributed to the revival of Taoism and the triumph of Buddhism. There were many Buddhist missionaries from India and central Asia. In addition Chinese made pilgrimages to the Buddhist countries. Many sects flourished at this time. Subsequently, Buddhism became the dominant intellectual force in China, followed by Taoism. Even those scholars who continued to accept the authority of the Confucian classics seem to have been deeply tinged with Taoism and Buddhism. But it must not be thought that Buddhism was free to expand unchecked. The suspicions of Confucian scholars and the jealousy of Taoists resulted in a number of minor and a few serious major persecutions of those who adopted the Buddhist faith. A sign of the times was the famous memorial on the subject of the Buddha's finger-bone presented to the throne in 819 by the great scholar and essayist Han Yü (768–824), in which he denounced Buddha as a "barbarian" and criticized the emperor for paying honor to such a savage relic as Buddha's finger-bone. This daring memorial caused Han Yü to be condemned to exile and nearly cost him his life.

Nevertheless, Han Yü was not utterly unrecompensed for his defense of the orthodox Confucian tradition against the inroads of Buddhist superstitions. Only some twenty years after his death, the court itself became so anti-Buddhist that the imperial edict of 845 resulted in the destruction of 4,600 Buddhist monasteries, the demolition of 40,000 Buddhist temples and shrines, the return of 265,000 of its devotees to secular life, the confiscation of monastic property to state uses, and the turning of sacrificial bells and ceremonial bronze vessels into cash. A severe blow to Buddhism indeed! A re-assertion of Chinese tradition.

For his defense of the great tradition, Han Yü was eulogized in the *Hsin T'ang Shu* (*New History of the T'ang Dynasty*):

> Of old, Mencius, who was only two hundred years removed from Confucius, had refuted Yang [Chu] and Mo [Ti]. [In the same way] Han Yü, though separated from Confucius by more than one thousand years, rejected the two schools [of Taoism and Buddhism]. In his destroying of confusion and restoring of orthodoxy, he equals [Mencius] in merit and doubles him in energy, thus surprising by not a little both K'uang [Hsün Tzu] and Hsiung [Yang Hsiung (53 B.C.–A.D. 18)].

In his famous essay entitled *Yüan Tao* ("On the Origin of Tao"), Han Yü wrote:

> What *Tao* is this? I say: This is what I call the *Tao*, and not what the Taoists and Buddhists call the *Tao*. This *Tao* Yao transmitted to Shun, Shun transmitted to Yü, Yü transmitted to T'ang. T'ang transmitted to Wen and Wu, and Duke Chou. These men handed it down to Confucius, who passed it on to Mencius. After the death of Mencius, it was no longer transmitted. Hsün Tzu and Yang Hsiung could make distinctions, but they were not sufficiently eminent; they could discuss it but not thoroughly.

This short passage makes three points clear: First, this *Tao* was not the mystical *Tao*, as conceived by the Taoists and Buddhists; it was, instead, a true way of life, which was handed down by early sage-rulers extending to Confucius and finally to Mencius. Second, the theory of an orthodox transmission of this *Tao* came to be accepted by the Sung and Ming Neo-Confucian scholars. Hence the new school of thought has been known as the *Tao Hsüeh Chia* (the School of the Learning of the *Tao*). Third, Han Yü paid high tribute to Mencius, assigning him an eminent place in the pantheon of Confucianism. He was particularly insistent on the "orthodox line of transmission" (*Tao-t'ung*) and rejected Hsün Tzu and Yang Hsiung as unworthy of it. This "orthodox line of transmission" has been generally accepted by Confucian scholars ever since.

In the *Yuan Tao*, Han Yü quoted at some length important passages from the *Ta Hsüeh* (*Great Learning*) for the exposition of the Confucian aim of life. As noted in our Chapter 5, this short treatise was originally one of the chapters in the *Li Chi* (*Book of Rites*). Since the Han dynasty few scholars had paid any attention to it. Han Yü, however, stressed that such phrases as "manifestation of illustrious virtue," "rectification of the mind" and "sincerity in thought," should be guiding principles in questions involving human life. The Neo-Confucian scholars also picked out these passages and unconsciously read into them Taoism and Buddhism. Thereupon the *Ta Hsüeh*, like the *Meng Tzu*, became an important text for Neo-Confucianism.

Another pioneer of the Neo-Confucian Movement was Li Ao (died *c.* 844), a contemporary of Han Yü. As an introspective thinker, Li Ao pondered the philosophical problems of the *Tao*. Much attention has been paid to his metaphysical speculations. His philosophical ideas were presented mostly in an essay entitled "*Fu-hsing Shu*" ("Recovery of Human Nature"), in which he said:

> The ancient sages transmitted this teaching to Master Yen [i.e. Yen Hui] . . . Tzu Ssu, the grandson of Confucius, re-

ceived the teaching of his grandfather, and composed the *Chung Yung* [the *Doctrine of the Mean*] in forty-seven sections, which he transmitted to Mencius. . . . The latter's disciples, . . . Kung-sun Ch'ou and Wan Chang, . . . transmitted it further. But when, under the Ch'in, the books were destroyed [in 213 B.C.], only one section of the *Chung Yung* survived the burning, and thereupon this teaching became obscured and incomplete. . . .

Then Li Ao quoted from the *Chung Yung* to illustrate his theory of human nature and destiny. The *Chung Yung*—originally one section of the *Li Chi*—was singled out for quotation by Li Ao, and thereafter, like the *Ta Hsüeh*, it also became an important text for Neo-Confucian philosophers.

The way of interpreting the Confucian classics, as noted in the *"Fu-hsing Shu"* is Confucian, but at the same time it clearly shows the influence of Buddhist doctrines. The preoccupation was still with human relations and moral values, but terms like *hsing* (nature), *ch'eng* (reality), *ming* (enlightenment), *wu* (things) and *chih* (wisdom) were brought into the foreground. In this way, Li Ao was more of an introspective thinker than Han Yü. He pondered the philosophical problems of the *Tao*, and his metaphysical speculations approached nearer to those of the Sung philosophers. Though he expounded his theory of human nature in Confucian terms, the Buddhist influence is evident.

Like Han Yü, Li Ao, despite the influence of Buddhism and Taoism, consciously rejected the heterodox teachings of these two rival schools. Thus he said in the *"Fu-hsing Shu"*:

> Alas! Though books about nature and destiny are still extant, nobody is interested in them. Everybody has joined the schools of Lao Tzu, the Buddha, Chuang Tzu and Lieh Tzu. They all believe that the followers of Confucius are not learned enough to know about nature and destiny, but that they themselves are. When someone once asked me about this, I did my best to expound reality (*ch'eng*) and enlightenment (*ming*). I hope that *Tao*, which has been obscured and neglected, may be

transmitted again. If Confucius came to life today he would not consider my talk worthless.

It is evident that Li Ao had a great mission; that is, the revival of Confucianism. This also reflects the motivation underlying the rise of Neo-Confucianism.

In the last analysis, the significance of Han Yü and Li Ao as pioneers of the Neo-Confucian movement lies in their attempt to reinterpret such works as the *Ta Hsüeh* and *Chung Yung* in such a way as would answer the philosophical problems of the *Tao* and the theory of human nature. However, it was not until the Sung epoch (960–1279) that a new system of thought was formed to satisfy the inquiring mind of the Chinese people, as stimulated by Buddhist—and Taoist—cosmology and metaphysics.

The Leading Sung Neo-Confucian Philosophers

In the work of setting anew the foundations of religion and philosophy, seven men of the Sung period took the lead: Chou Tun-i (1017–73), Shao Yung (1011–77), Chang Tsai (1020–77), Ch'eng Hao (1032–85), Ch'eng I (1033–1107), Chu Hsi (1130–1200), and Lu Hsiang-shan (1139–93). All the leading Neo-Confucian thinkers were no doubt Confucian scholars, but by nature or by training they were predisposed to cosmological speculations of Buddhist and Taoist writers. Their writings derive immense importance from the fact that they began to ponder the philosophical problems dealing with the origin of the universe, the external world, and man as a part of the universe. With answers to these problems Chinese philosophy passed from its ancient to its modern period.

Let us now consider the first of these seven leading Neo-Confucian scholars who contributed substantially to the new movement: Chou Tun-i, a cosmologist. Chou Tun-i, together with Shao Yung and Chang Tsai, formed the great trio in the first stage of the Neo-Confucian development.

Chou Tun-i (also known as Chou Lien-hsi) was considered the founder of Neo-Confucianism. He composed two short treatises: the *T'ai-chi-tu Shuo* (*An Explanation of the Diagram of the Supreme Ultimate*) and the *T'ung-shu* (*Book of Comprehensive Understanding*). In fact, the former is a part of the latter. Chou Tun-i took from the *Book of Changes* the term "Supreme Ultimate" and devised a cosmological diagram, a formula (probably of Taoist origin) showing how *yin* and *yang* and the "five elements" derived from this "Supreme Ultimate."

The text of the *T'ai-chi-tu Shuo* reads as follows:

The ultimateless [*Wu-chi*]! And yet the Supreme Ultimate [*T'ai-chi*]! The Supreme Ultimate through Movement produces the *Yang*. This Movement, having reached its limit, is followed by Quiescence (*Ching*), and by this Quiescence it produces the *Yin*. When Quiescence has reached its limit, there is a return to Movement. Thus Movement and Quiescence, in alternation, become each the source of the other. The distinction between the *Yin* and *Yang* is determined, and the Two Forms [*i.e.*, the *Yin* and *Yang*] are established.

By the transformation of the *Yang* and the union therewith of the *Yin*, Water, Fire, Wood, Metal, and Earth are produced. These Five Vital Forces [*ch'i*, *i.e.*, elements] are distributed in harmonious order, and the four seasons proceed in their course.

The Five Elements constitute the one *Yin* and *Yang*, and the *Yin* and *Yang* constitute the one Supreme Ultimate. The Supreme Ultimate is fundamentally the Ultimateless. The Five Elements arise, each with its specific nature.

The truth of the Ultimateless and the essence of the Two [Forms] and Five [Elements] are mysteriously integrated and so consolidated. The *Tao* [principle] of *Chi'en* [the hexagram ☰ symbolizing the *Yang*] becomes the male element, and the *Tao* of *K'un* [the hexagram ☷ symbolizing the *Yin*] becomes the female element. The two Vital Forces (*Yin* and *Yang*) by their interaction operate to produce the myriad

things, and the myriad things in their turn produce and repro-
duce, so that transformation and change continue without end.

This is his theory of the creation and evolution of the universe,
generally accepted by later scholars. The second part of the
T'ai-chi-tu Shuo deals with the ethical theory of Chou Tun-i:

> Man alone, however, receives the Vital Forces [*ch'i*] in their
> highest excellence, and therefore he is most intelligent. His
> physical form being thus produced, consciousness is developed
> in spirit. The five principles of his nature react [to external
> world], so that good and evil are distinguished, and all kinds
> of action take place.
>
> The sage regulates himself by [the principles of] *Chung*
> [the Mean], *Cheng* [the Correct], *Jen* [Human-heartedness]
> and *I* [Righteousness], regarding Quiescence as the essential.
> Thus he establishes himself as the highest standard for man-
> kind.

This is to show that man is regarded as the highest of all creations, and the sage the greatest of all men. Then the treatise
continues:

> Therefore, the sage coordinates with Heaven and Earth in
> his nature, with the sun and moon in his enlightenment, with
> the course of the seasons in his orderliness, and with the
> spiritual beings in his fortune. The superior man, by cultivating
> these [virtues of the sage] enjoys good fortune, whereas the
> inferior man, by violating them, incurs bad fortune.

It is evident that Chou Tun-i aimed at personal cultivation
toward the end of being in harmony with the universe. Then
the treatise concludes:

> The *Tao* of Heaven is established by the *Yin* and *Yang;* the
> *Tao* of Earth is established by softness and hardness; the *Tao*
> of Man is established by *jen* and *yi*. By tracing to the beginning
> and reverting to the end, one shall know the meaning of life
> and death. Great is the *I* [*Book of Changes*]! Herein lies its
> ultimate truth.

In conclusion, Chou Tun-i based his entire philosophy on the *Book of Changes*. What happens in the universe he traced back to the Supreme Ultimate, the *Yin* and *Yang*, and the Five Elements, all for the purpose of illustrating the significance of the *Tao*. Meanwhile, he stressed the ideas of *jen* and *yi*, and recommended Quiescence as the proper approach to that ideal of sagehood elaborated in the *Tung-shu* (which quotes much from the *Chung Yung*). All these ideas, which were accepted by later Confucian scholars, undoubtedly contributed to the development of Neo-Confucianism and Chou Tun-i was rightly considered the founder of the Sung Neo-Confucianism.

The second proponent of the Sung philosophy to be mentioned here is Shao Yung (also known as Shao K'ang-chieh). Like most of his contemporaries, Shao Yung had been a student of Taoism and Buddhism before he turned to Confucianism. He was a mystic and much of his thinking had a Taoist origin. He was not as much concerned with social and moral problems as were his fellow Neo-Confucian scholars. On account of this he had been considered as relatively unorthodox by scholars who were brought up in Confucian tradition. However, his writings testify to the breadth of his knowledge and the profundity of his cosmological speculations. His most important work is *Huang-chi ching-shih shu* (Cosmological Chronology), especially the chapters on "the Observation of Things" (*Kuan-wu P'ien*).

Like Chou Tun-i, Shao Yung developed his cosmological theory on the basis of the *I Ching*, making deft use of diagrams to illustrate his theory. But Shao Yung went further back than Chou Tun-i to the very fountain head of metaphysics. Chou Tun-i's *T'ai-chi-tu shuo*, we know, is a study of symbols as found in the *I Ching*, whereas Shao Yung's *Huang-chi ching-shih shu* combines symbols with numbers so as to present the basic concept of the *I* (*Chang*). Here is a passage from the *Kuan-wu P'ien*:

> The Supreme Ultimate is One and unmoving. It produces Two [*yin* and *yang*]. The Two constitute Spirit [*shen*].

Spirit produces Numbers, the Numbers produce Symbols, and the Symbols produce material objects.

In this short passage it is asserted that the whole process of cosmic evolution begins with the Supreme Ultimate, goes through Numbers and Symbols, and finally culminates in material objects. These Numbers and Symbols are illustrated in the Primeval Diagram (*Hsien-t'ien-tu*), as worked out by Shao Yung. This Diagram represents in fact a formula for the life cycle of the myriad creatures in their birth, growth, maturity, decline and death. More interesting, Shao Yung also applied his theory of numbers, with its diagram to the chronology of the universe, dividing the history of the universe into Cosmic Periods and classifying historical events according to numerical categories. According to Shao Yung, what happens in the universe can be represented by symbols (the sixty-four hexagrams of the *I Ching*) and at the same time can be predicted by mathematical calculation.

Since he was devoted to cosmological and numerical studies, Shao Yung believed in eternal truth and was, therefore, insistent on the "objective viewing of things." This is what is written in the *Kuan-wu P'ien*:

> By viewing things is not meant viewing them with one's eye. No, it is not viewing with one's eye, but with one's mind. Nor is it viewing with one's mind, but with the "principle inherent in things (*li*)." [1] There is nothing in the universe that does not have its own principle (*li*), nature (*hsing*) and destiny (*ming*). These can be known only when principle has been investigated to the utmost, when the nature has been completely developed and when destiny has been fulfilled. The knowledge of these three is the real knowledge of the world, and even the sage cannot go beyond it. Whoever goes beyond it cannot be called a sage.

Although his theory of numbers, with its various diagrams, was probably too complicated and abstruse to have had any important influence on his contemporaries, yet his concepts of principle, destiny and nature are characteristic of Neo-Confucian thought. Even more important, Shao Yung, true to Confucian tradition, placed much emphasis on man. In the *Kuan-wu P'ien* we read:

> The *Tao* is the basis of Heaven and Earth, and Heaven and Earth are the bases of the myriad things. Viewed from Heaven and Earth, the myriad things are the myriad things. When Heaven and Earth are viewed from the *Tao*, then Heaven and Earth themselves are also the myriad things. The principle of the *Tao* finds its full development in Heaven; the principle of Heaven and Earth, in the myriad things; the principle of the myriad things in the universe, in man. One who knows how and why the principle of the myriad things in the universe find their development in man can give full development to his people.

This is the sort of passage one wants to re-read but Shao Yung is clearer as to the reason why all things in the universe find their full development in man. The *Kuan-wu P'ien* continues:

> Man is the most intelligent of all things because his eyes can perceive the colors of the myriad things, his ears can listen to all kinds of sounds, his nose can smell all sorts of odors, and his mouth can distinguish the tastes of food. Colors, sounds, smells, and tastes are the substance of the myriad things, and ears, eyes, nose and mouth are the functions of all men. Substance has no definite function, but its function is to transform itself. Function, again, has no definite substance, but its substance is [cosmic] change itself. In the mutual stimulation of substance and function, the *Tao* of man and the physical world is completely fulfilled.

This passage also helps to explain that man's intelligence does not rely upon sense-knowledge, but rather on the mind that is devoted to research in the *Tao* (that is, eternal truth). Then the same treatise continues:

We know, therefore, that man is the highest of all creatures, and that a sage is the highest of men. The highest of men is he who can view myriad other minds by one mind, who can view myriad other bodies by one body, who can view myriad other objects by one object, and who can view myriad other generations by one generation. It is also he who can represent the will of Heaven with his mind, who can represent the speech of Heaven with his mouth, who can represent the work of Heaven with his hand, and who can represent the functions of Heaven with his body. This means that he is man who knows the seasons of Heaven above, who comprehends the principles of Earth below, and, between these, the nature of things and the affairs of mankind. That is to say, he is man who can supplement and carry forward [the work of] Heaven and Earth, who can proceed with the process of creation, who can be well versed in the past and in the present, and who can make choice of men.

According to Shao Yung, man is the most intelligent of all living creatures, and the ideal man is the sage who is guided by the principle of Heaven. Shao's metaphysical approach made him less Confucian and more Taoist but in fairness Shao Yung should be considered as a challenging and refreshing thinker within the fold of the Sung philosophy or beyond it, even though he exercised little influence on his contemporaries and had virtually no followers. His vast mental horizon and keen interest in mathematics and cosmological study will be more appreciated in this age of scientific and philosophical progress than it was in earlier times.

The third great philosopher of the Sung period to be mentioned here is Chang Tsai (also know as Chang Heng-ch'ü). Chang Tsai, like those who preceded him, developed a cosmological theory from the *I Ching* (Appendix III). However, his starting point was different from that of his predecessors Chou Tun-i and Shao Yung. The term "Supreme Ultimate," originated by Chou Tun-i, now became the focus of philosophical discussion by the Sung philosophers. But as to the meaning of the Supreme Ultimate, opinions were sharply divided. In Shao

Yung's writings, for instance, it was often referred to as the *Tao*, the mind, or the nature. But to Chang Tsai, the Supreme Ultimate was nothing more than the *Ch'i* (vital force or ether), a concept which, together with the *Li* (principle), became more and more important in the cosmological and metaphysical theories of the later Neo-Confucian scholars.

Chang Tsai regarded the *Ch'i* as the basic element in all things. The *Ch'i* in its entirety he called the *T'ai-ho* (Supreme Harmony), or alternately, the *Tao*. In his famous work, the *Cheng Meng* (*Corrections of Youthful Ignorance*), there is a passage on this subject in his chapter on the *T'ai-ho*:

> The *T'ai-ho* is called the *Tao;* inherent in this is the nature which underlies all interacting processes of floating and sinking, rising and falling, moving and being still. Here also appears the beginning of the mutual stimulation of overcoming and being overcome, and of contraction and expansion.

Chang Tsai says that within this *Ch'i* is included the *Yin* and the *Yang*. The *Ch'i*, when dominated by the *Yin* element, tends to sink, to fall, and to be still, while the *Ch'i*, when dominated by the *Yang* element, tends to float, to rise, and to move. Because of the interaction, the *Ch'i* is thrown continuously into "floating and sinking, rising and falling," without being able to remain static in a state of void.

There is good reason for this. In Chang Tsai's opinion, it is the *Ch'i* which forms the *T'ai-hsü* (Great Void) which has no physical shape and yet contains the substance of all existing things. So he writes:

> The *Ch'i*'s condensation from and dispersion into the *T'ai-hsü* is like ice's freezing from and melting into water. Once we realize that the *T'ai-hsü* is the same as the *Ch'i*, there is no non-existence (*Wu*) (*ibid.*).

According to Chang Tsai, the *Ch'i* has the attributes of both condensing and dispersing. Thus the condensation of the *Ch'i* results in the formation of objects; its dispersion results in their dissolution. And because of the endless condensation and dispersion, myriad objects are formed and dissolved. Chang Tsai writes:

> When the *Ch'i* condenses, its visibility becomes apparent and hence there are shapes. But when the *Ch'i* disperses, its visibility is no longer apparent and hence there are no shapes. At the time of its condensation, can one say otherwise than that this is but temporary? But at the time of its dispersion, can one conclude hastily that it is non-existent (*Wu*)? Therefore, the sage, after he has gazed aloft and looked below, only asserts that he knows the cause of visibility and invisibility, but not the cause of existence (*Yü*) and non-existence (*Wu*) (*ibid.*).

Having discussed his cosmological theory, let us turn to Chang Tsai's ethics, as illustrated in his short treatise *Hsi-ming* (*Western Inscription*). The significance of Chang Tsai as a great Sung philosopher lies largely in the *Hsi-ming*, which has become the basis of Neo-Confucian ethics. It reads as follows:

Ch'ien [☰] is called the father, and *K'un* [☷] is called the mother. I, as a tiny being, live in the midst of them. Therefore, the Plenum of Heaven and Earth I regard as my body; the Pilot of Heaven and Earth I consider as my nature. All people are my brothers; all things are my companions. The Great Ruler [Emperor] is the eldest son of my parents [Heaven and Earth], and his great ministers are the household retainers. To respect the aged means to treat them as elders should be treated. To be kind to the orphaned and the weak means to treat them as the young should be treated. The sage is one who is equal to Heaven and Earth in virtue, and the worthy is the most gifted among men. All those who are overworked, crippled, infirm, or sick; those who are brotherless, childless, widowers, or widows,—are all my brothers who are in distress and have none to whom they can appeal. To protect them at the proper time constitutes a son's responsibility [toward Heaven]. To rejoice [in Heaven] and to have no anxiety means to exemplify filial piety in all its purity.

One who deviates from this [principle] violates virtue; one who injures *jen* [human-heartedness] is a robber. One who assists the evil-doing lacks merits, whereas one who fulfills his mission is said to match [Heaven and Earth]. One who knows the changes [of the universe] will carry forward skillfully the activities [of Heaven and Earth]. One who comprehends the spiritual thoroughly will follow the purpose [of Heaven and Earth]. One who even in the recesses of one's own house does nothing shameful, will bring no shame to anyone. One who preserves one's mind and nourishes one's nature, will not be negligent. . . .

Wealth, honor, fortune, and happiness are meant for the enrichment of my life. However, poverty, humbleness, grief, and sorrow are meant to discipline me for success. In life I shall serve [Heaven and Earth], and in death I shall be at peace.

In this short treatise, two salient points are made. First, it stresses the unity of man with Heaven, thus underscoring the need of obliterating all distinction between the ego and the non-ego. Since all things in the universe are constituted of one and the same *Ch'i*, it is to be expected that there is a great deal in common not only among men themselves but also between men and the other creatures. In particular, our own body is the body of the universe, and our individual nature is identical with that of the universe. Second, it expounds the theory of *jen*. But Chang Tsai went much further than that. His concept of *jen*, as illustrated in the *Hsi-ming*, is not just the Confucian concept of a graded love; it is rather akin to the discredited Mohist concept of an all-embracing love (*chien ai*) that is equal and undiscriminating for all. Moreover, Confucian *jen* had been largely conceived in terms of the mundane world because of its emphasis on human relationships. Chang Tsai, however, extended it to encompass the whole universe, including Heaven, Earth, men and the myriad creatures. He maintained that we should regard Heaven and Earth (*i.e., Ch'ien* and *K'un,* personified as the universal parents) as our own parents and serve them in the same manner as we do our own parents. Moreover, we should, he asserts, regard all men of the world as our own brothers and all creatures as our own kind. In so doing he extended the ethical concept of *jen* to embrace cosmic significance, which may be attributed to the influence of Buddhism. Nevertheless, the last statement in the *Hsi-ming* ("In life I shall serve [Heaven and Earth], and in death I shall be at peace") remains true to Confucian attitudes toward life and death—an attitude that had been followed by the Neo-Confucian scholars of the Sung and Ming periods. In short, this brief treatise, the *Hsi-ming*, has been considered one of the most important documents of Sung philosophy, because of the ethical implications of its cosmic love by its emphasis on the family relationship, although its application is analogical.

Following the cosmological speculations of Chou Tun-i, Shao Yung and Chang Tsai, came the two Ch'eng brothers—Ch'eng Hao and Ch'eng I—who turned the trend of Chinese thought from cosmology to the study of ethical and epistemological problems. It is interesting to note that the two Ch'eng brothers were students of Chou Tun-i, friends of Shao Yung and nephews of Chang Tsai. They were often mentioned together as the "Two Ch'eng Masters," because their recorded conversations were handed down under a common authorship, namely, *Erh-Ch'eng I-shu* (*Surviving Works of the Two Ch'engs*) and little effort was made to distinguish the work of one from the other. In fact the two Ch'engs seemed to be not only different in their temperaments but also in their philosophical thought, which foreshadowed the two major trends of Neo-Confucianism: the Rationalistic Neo-Confucianism and the Idealistic Neo-Confucianism. These two trends of Neo-Confucianism will be taken up later. Here let us examine the "Two Ch'eng Masters."

The great contribution made by the Ch'eng brothers was the introduction of *Li* (principle, or the eternal law) as an important concept in the new philosophy. The concept of *Li* is not a unique element in the teachings of the Ch'engs, for it had been used by their predecessors. We have mentioned it above in connection with Shao Yung. However, it was the

Ch'eng brothers who first made the *Li* the foundation of Sung philosophy, sometimes known as *Li-Hsüeh* (*Philosophy of Principle*). According to these two great Neo-Confucian scholars, the *Li* is an intangible cosmic principle to be distinguished from the *Ch'i* (ether or vital force), of which all material things are made. For them, "the *Li* lies in the myriad things of the world." In other words, all things in the world, if they are to exist at all, must embody some principle in some material. The principle is what they call *Li*, and the material is what they call *Ch'i*, Though they fixed on the *Li* and *Ch'i* as the seminal elements of the universe, each involving the other, yet, the *Li* is prior to and independent of the *Ch'i* in which it manifests itself. In the *Erh-Ch'eng I-shu* we read:

> "All things are already complete in oneself." (*Meng Tzu* VIIA–4). This statement applies not only to man but to all other creatures; they all act in accordance with this (*Li*). The only thing is that whereas these other creatures cannot extend (the *Li* in them), man can. Even though man can extend it, does this mean that it has been slightly increased? And though (other creatures) cannot extend it, does this mean that it has been slightly diminished? The (*Li*) is pervasively present. Can one say that Yao (Legendary Sage ruler), in fulfilling the *Tao* of rulership, added anything to it? Or did Shun [Yao's successor noted for his filial piety], in fulfilling the *Tao* of sonship, add anything to it? For the *Li* always remains what it is.

And again:

> There is only one *Li* in the world, which, though extending to [all within] the four seas, remains true. It ever remains an unchanging principle that "can be brought before Heaven and Earth" and be "tested by the experience of the Three Kings [who founded the Hsia, Shang and Chou dynasties] . . . As to this *Li*, the *jen*-hearted see it and call it *jen*. The wise see it and call it wisdom. The common people use it daily, yet without realizing it. This is why the *Tao* of the Superior Man is seldom seen. This *Li* itself, however, is neither diminished

nor preserved; the fact is that men fail to perceive it. . . . "Being silent and inactive, becoming activated, thereupon to penetrate everywhere and all things" [*I Ching*, appen. III]—such is the *T'ien-li* [Heavenly Principle], which is self-sufficient and in which there is fundamentally no deficiency. It did not survive because of Yao, nor did it cease to exist because of Chieh [a wicked ruler]. The constant *Li* governing [the relationships of] father and son, ruler and minister, remains unchanged (*ibid.*).

According to the Ch'eng brothers, the *Li* is universal and eternal, and can neither be added to nor diminished. It makes no difference whether men know of it or not. The sage Yao, for instance, in fulfilling the *Tao* of rulership, set up a concrete example of it, but the *Li* of the rulership was not increased. This is why the Ch'engs say that "the *Li* is pervasively present."

The second characteristic of *Li*, as conceived by the Ch'eng brothers, is that the *Li* remains unchanged and indestructible. In other words, the *Li* is always the same. This is why the *Li* "did not survive because of Yao, nor did it cease to exist because of Chieh." Good rulers and tyrants come and go and the *Li* remains forever.

The third point is that the *Li*, as it is described, is "silent and inactive," and yet when "activated, it penetrates everywhere and all things." In other words, the *Li*, being self-evident and self-sufficient, transcends shapes and features.

Up to this point, we find that the two Ch'eng brothers were agreed. But they differed in other questions to which they devoted themselves. True to Confucian tradition, they maintained that learning is to begin with cultivation to be a scholar and end with attainment as a sage. But as to the correct approach to the sage ideal, it seems the Ch'eng brothers disagreed. Since Ch'eng Hao (also called Ch'eng Ming-tao), the elder, greatly admired Chang Tsai's *Hsi-ming*, it was to be expected that he would place emphasis on the virtue of *jen* as the ideal of the perfect individual. In the *Erh-Ch'eng I-shu*, Ch'eng Hao says:

The student must first comprehend *jen*. The man of *jen* is undifferentially one with all things. *Yi* (righteousness), *li* (propriety), *chih* (wisdom), and *hsin* (good faith): all these are *jen*. Get to comprehend this *Li* and preserve [*jen*] with sincerity (*ch'eng*) and seriousness (*ching*), that is all. There is no need for restraint or for exhaustive search. It is necessary to restrict oneself when one's mind is negligent. Otherwise, why is there need for restraint? Exhaustive search is necessary, when the *Li* has not yet been grasped. After one becomes familiar with it, why need one search for it? . . . [As Mencius said in *Meng Tzu* IIA–2], "as if you were devoted to something but that this something requires no correction. The mind should not be negligent, and you should not try to help growth." [The significance of this remark is that] no extra effort is needed. This is the way to preserve *jen*. When *jen* is preserved, the self and the other are united. For the *liang chih* [intuitive knowledge] and the *liang neng* [intuitive ability] are born with you, and cannot be lost. As long as the old habits have not been discarded, it is necessary to exercise vigilance over the mind. By the proper maintenance the old habits will be overcome. This *Li* is rather simple. The important point is to hold to it. Once having experienced the delight of embodying it, there will be no fear of being unable to hold to it (IIA).

The above passage on the theory of spiritual cultivation, based on the Confucian doctrine of *jen*, has been as important in Neo-Confucianism as Chang Tsai's *Hsi-ming*. According to Ch'eng Hao, the meaning of *jen* is that one should feel oneness with the whole universe. This feeling is something inherent in man's nature. It often happens, however, that one's innate feeling is obscured by selfish desires, and the union of man with the universe is lost. The main purpose of spiritual cultivation is therefore to extend oneself to include others, so as to return to the original state of universal oneness. This is carried out by remembering the original oneness between oneself and the universe and by acting accordingly with sincerity and seriousness. These ideas were later followed by Lu Hsiang-shan (1139–

93) and Wang Shou-jen (1472–1528) to develop the *Hsin Hsüeh* school, or School of the Study of Mind, also known as the Idealistic Neo-Confucianism.

Ch'eng I (also called Ch'eng I-ch'uan), the younger, agreed with Ch'eng Hao on the importance of spiritual cultivation. But the approach of Ch'eng I to the problem was along more rationalistic lines. Ch'eng I was more emphatic in stressing knowledge of the physical world, whereas Ch'eng Hao's starting point was the ideal of *jen*. In the *Erh-Ch'eng I-shu* there is a statement attributed to Ch'eng I:

> For [spiritual] cultivation, one needs *ching* [seriousness]; for the advancement of learning, one needs *chih chih* [the extension of knowledge] (*chüan* 18).

It is interesting to note that Ch'eng I, like Ch'eng Hao, by stressing seriousness in the process of spiritual cultivation, deviates from Chou Tun-i, who, as mentioned above, recommended Quiescence as the approach to the sage-ideal. The agreement between the two Ch'eng brothers ends there, howver. The important aspect of Ch'eng I's approach centers around the two terms taken from the *Ta Hsüeh* (the *Great Learning*): *chih chih* ("extension of knowledge") and *ko wu* ("investigation of things"). Let us quote from the *Erh-Ch'eng I-shu*:

> Someone asked what should come first in the art of spiritual cultivation. [Ch'eng I answered:] There is nothing more primary than rectifying the mind and making the purpose sincere. The sincerity of the purpose lies in the extension of knowledge (*chih chih*), and the extension of knowledge lies in the investigation of things (*ko wu*). . . . There is *Li* in everything, and one must make exhaustive study of *Li*. There are many ways of doing this: one may read books and expound their meaning; one may discourse on personages of the past and present, distinguishing the right and the wrong; or one may manage affairs and settle them in the proper way. All

these are ways of making the exhaustive study of *Li* (*chüan* 18).

According to Ch'eng I, the process of spiritual cultivation starts with the exhaustive study of *Li*, which is to be regarded as something pertaining to knowledge. In this way he not only placed emphasis on the concept of *Li* but also provided a rational basis for Sung philosophy. Indeed he was the first of the Sung philosophers to attach importance to the intellectual process as distinct from intuitive knowledge. In this respect he was later followed by Chu Hsi (1130–1200). Together they found the Ch'eng-Chu school (sometimes known as the *Li Hsüeh* school) which was Rationalistic Neo-Confucianism.

Another difference between the two Ch'eng brothers lies in their interpretation of a statement in "Appendix III" of the *I Ching*: "That which is above shape is called the *Tao*; that which is below shape is called the implement." According to Ch'eng I's interpretation of this, the *Li*, as the eternal principle that transcends time and space, belongs to the first category, that is, "above shape," while the *Ch'i* as manifested in concrete objects belongs to the second category, that is, "below shape." But Ch'eng Hao seemed to disagree with his brother. The *Li*, for Ch'eng Hao, is nothing more than a natural tendency inherent in any concrete object, and as such cannot exist apart from an object. Thus he wrote: "The *Li*, which lies in the myriad things, never stands singly, but is one of a pair of opposites. This is nature's way" (*chuan* 2). He stressed that "everything comes in opposites. The *Yin* has the *Yang* as its counterpart." (*Ibid.*) He also observed: "The implement is the *Tao*, and the *Tao* the implement" (*Ibid.*).

Therefore, in Ch'eng Hao's system of thought, there is little distinction between the spheres of "what is above shape" (the metaphysical) and of "what is below shape" (the physical). This monistic theory came to be generally accepted by the *Hsin Hsüeh* school.

We must note one more difference between the two brothers, in regard to the theory of human nature (*hsing*). As regards the meaning of the term *hsing* (nature), the opening sentence of the *Chung Yung* reads: "That which Heaven confers is called the nature." And again, in the *Meng Tzu* (VIA–3) we find: "Kao Tzu said: 'That which comes with life is the nature.'" But the Sung philosophers tended to associate the nature with the *Ch'i* or *Li*. In the words of Chang Tsai:

> From the Great Void is derived the term *Heaven*. From the transformation of the *Ch'i* is derived the term *Tao*. From the combination of the Void with the *Ch'i* is derived the term *nature* (*hsing*). From the combination of the nature with consciousness is derived the term *mind* (the *Cheng Meng* 2.7).

This thought is prominent in the writings of Sung philosophers. A similar statement is found in the *Erh-Ch'eng I-shu*:

> "That which comes with life is the nature." The nature is the same as the *Ch'i*, and the *Ch'i* is the same as the nature. They both come with life (*chüan* 1).

Though the text does not indicate the authorship of the statement, it is generally attributed to Ch'eng Hao. Then Ch'eng Hao explained that while human nature in its origin is good, after man's birth he is endowed with the *Ch'i*. But the *Ch'i* may be either good or evil, just as water may be either pure or impure. Only by self-cultivation, therefore, can the nature which has become evil be restored to its original goodness with which man is endowed prior to his birth.

Ch'eng I identified human nature with the *Li*, which "from its very beginning cannot be other than good." Hence he believed in the theory of the goodness of human nature and said in the *Erh-Ch'eng I-shu*:

> The nature comes from Heaven, whereas capacity comes from the *Ch'i*. When the *Ch'i* is clear, capacity is clear. When the *Ch'i* is turbid, capacity is turbid. . . . Capacity may be good or evil, but the nature is always good (*Chüan* 19).

And again:

> That which pertains to Heaven is the *ming* (Destiny); that
> which pertains to righteousness is the *Li;* that which pertains to
> man is the nature; that which is the ruler of the body is the
> mind. These, in fact, are all one. The mind itself is originally
> good, but as it is manifested in its expression, it is sometimes
> good, and sometimes evil. What is thus manifested may be
> called feelings, and not the mind itself (*chüan* 18).

For Ch'eng I, the mind, the nature, and the *Li* are always
good. In this respect, just as comprehension of the *Li* lies in the
rectification of the mind, so the complete development of the
nature lies in the comprehension of the *Li*. Here is the essence
of Ch'eng I's theory that human nature is the *Li*. This theory,
however, has been rejected by the *Hsin Hsüeh* school on the
grounds that in human nature there are emotions and desires,
which are not reducible to the one source, the *Li*.

The last two leading Neo-Confucian philosophers of the
Sung period—Chu Hsi and Lo Hsiang-shan—will be taken up
in the following chapter as we outline the two main trends of
Neo-Confucianism.

CHAPTER **8**

The Diversity of
Neo-Confucianism

Considerable diversity of thought among the Neo-Confucian thinkers ultimately led to the emergence within Neo-Confucianism of two major schools: Rationalism and Idealism. The Chinese call the former the *Li Hsüeh* (principle-study) school, developed by Ch'eng I (1033–1107) and Chu Hsi (1130–1200) and also known as the *Ch'eng-Chu* school, and the latter, the *Hsin Hsüeh* (mind-study) school, developed by Lu Hsiang-shan (1139–93) and Wang Yang-ming (1472–1529) and also known as the *Lu-Wang* school. Generally speaking, the Rationalistic Neo-Confucianism is nearer to the whole rationale of Confucian thought, and the Idealistic Neo-Confucianism is more akin to the thought of *Ch'an* (*Zen*) Buddhism. These two divergent schools differ widely in ideology and methodology. The ideological controversy between the two groups, which brings up many broadly important problems in philosophical thought, raged until the twentieth century. The *Hsin Hsüeh* school accused the *Li Hsüeh* school of being inspired by Taoism; the *Li Hsüeh* school retorted that the doctrine of its accuser abandoned Confucian teaching for Buddhism. In fact, both schools were influenced by both Taoism and Buddhism.

Rationalistic Neo-Confucianism

The leader of the *Li Hsüeh* school was Chu Hsi, better known as Chu Tzu or Master Chu, the most influential Chinese philosopher and the most voluminous writer during the last thousand years. He was born several decades after the Ch'eng brothers, and in consequence, was able to gather the harvest of these predecessors. Chu Hsi's real greatness lies in his synthesizing Chou Tun-i's *T'ai-chi-tu Shuo*, Shao Yung's *Hsien-t'ien-tu*, Chang Tsai's *Hsi-ming*, and the ideas of the Ch'eng brothers into one all-embracing system of thought. What he accomplished was not merely to appropriate the best thought of all these predecessors, but, on the basis of all previous thought, to build up a great system of philosophy, known as *Li Hsüeh*. It dominated Chinese thought for centuries.

Chu Hsi combined the best qualities of the laborious scholar and the acute thinker. He had a comprehensive knowledge and great ability to make it his own. His complete works, in sixty-two volumes, cover almost all Chinese learning, including the classics, history, philosophy, and literature.[1] His commentaries on the *Four Sacred Books* (the *Lun-yu, Meng Tzu, Ta Hsüeh* and *Chung Yung* as the central scriptures of Confucianism) and other classics were officially recognized, during the Ming (1368–1644) and Ch'ing (1644–1911) dynasties, as the standard texts required of all candidates in the state examination. He also introduced interpretations into the Confucian classics either wholly or partly at variance with those that had been put forth by the scholars of the Han period, thus modifying to a certain extent the prevailing standard of political and social morality. As a result, his influence on these classics became so significant that they were studied solely in the light of his interpretation.

In synthesizing the ideas of his predecessors into a comprehensive system of thought, metaphysical as well as ethical, Chu Hsi started by making the distinction established by Ch'eng I—

and also Ch'eng Hao—between "what is above shapes" (*i.e.*, the metaphysical) and "what is below shapes" (*i.e.*, the physical), as well as between the *Li* and the *Ch'i*. He considered the *Ch'i* as pertaining to "what is below shapes" and the *Li* as pertaining to "what is above shapes." Thus he said:

> Within Heaven and Earth, there is the *Li* and there is the *Ch'i*. The *Li* constitutes the *Tao*, which is above shapes; it is the source from which all things are produced. The *Ch'i* constitutes the implement, which is below shapes; it is the tool by which all things are produced. Hence men and things, at the moment of their production, must be endowed with the *Li* before they can have their inherent nature; they must be endowed with the *Ch'i* before they can have their physical form (*Answer to Huang Tao-fu*, the *Collected Works*, 58).

In other words, the *Li* pertains to the metaphysical world (or the "world above shapes") that is invisible, incorporeal, transcendental, and yet inherent in everything and pervading everything. The *Ch'i* pertains to the physical world (or the "world below shapes," out of which all things are created) that is visible, corporeal, and concrete. Thus Chu Hsi made a clearer distinction between the two inherent forces in the universe, the *Ch'i* and the *Li*.

> The *Ch'i* has the capacity to condense and thus create, whereas the *Li* lacks volition or plan and has no creative power. However, whenever the *Ch'i* condenses and coheres, the *Li* is present within it. Moreover, within Heaven and Earth, no human beings, plants, trees, birds and beasts can be produced save through [genetic] propagation. . . . This all pertains to the *Ch'i*. The *Li*, on the other hand, constitutes only a pure, empty, and vast world, utterly shapeless, and yet cannot create, whereas the *Ch'i* has the capacity to ferment and condense and thus produces things (*Yü Lei*, or *Classified Recorded Sayings*, 1).

As to whether there is a priority between the *Li* and the *Ch'i*, Chu Hsi said:

Fundamentally, [the *Li* and the *Ch'i*] cannot be spoken of as having either priority or posteriority. However, if one must trace their origin, one is obliged to admit that the *Li* has priority (ibid.).

Before the existence of Heaven-and-Earth, there was only the *Li*. There being the *Li*, this Heaven-and-Earth then came into existence. If there were no *Li*, there would be no Heaven-and-Earth, no human beings, and no things. . . . When there is the *Li*, there is the *Ch'i*, which flows into movement to produce the myriad things (ibid.).

Moreover, Chu Hsi maintained that the sum total of all the *Li* is the Supreme Ultimate (*T'ai Chi*), that is, the ultimate standard of Heaven and Earth and all things. As is found in the *Yü Lei* (ibid., 94):

For every thing or object there is an Ultimate, which is the universal *Li* in its ultimate form. . . . For instance, the *jen* of the sovereign and reverence of the minister are, then, such Ultimates. The Master [Chu Hsi] said: "This is the Ultimate of a single thing or object, the sum total of the *Li* in all the myriad things within Heaven-and-Earth constitutes the Supreme Ultimate."

The Supreme Ultimate, therefore, as the sum total of all the *Li*, is the highest standard of Heaven and Earth and all things. This being the case, "the Supreme Ultimate is simply an utterly excellent and supremely normative Principle [*Li*] " *Yü Lei* (94).

As noted above, in Chu Hsi's system, the *Li* is "the source from which all things are produced," and the *Ch'i* is "the tool by which all things are produced." In this respect, man, like all other creatures, is "the union of the *Li* with the *Ch'i*. This *Li*, which is combined with the *Ch'i* to produce an individual man, is then known as human nature (*hsing*). Hence the *Li* is the same for all men, and is always good. The *Ch'i*, however, is differentiated into the pure and the impure; hence it is in their *Ch'i* that men are different. In other words, one who receives the *Ch'i* that is pure, becomes a sage, whose nature is like a pearl lying in cold, translucent water. But one who receives the *Ch'i* that is impure will become a fool or a knave, whose nature is like a pearl lying in a muddy water. Here is the essence of Chu Hsi's view about the problem of human nature. Much controversy had arisen in the past among the Confucian scholars as to the moral quality of human nature. As we have seen, to Mencius human nature was good; to Hsün Tzu it was evil. The third view, as held by Yang Hsiang (53 B.C.–A.D.18), was that human nature was neither good nor evil but a mixture of the two. To solve the problem Chu Hsi devised a theory somewhat similar to Plato's account of the origin of evil. It clearly partakes of the three systems referred to above: in accordance with the first, it admits the original goodness of human nature (one's *Li*), at the same time admitting, with the second, that it contains some elements of evil (the impure *Ch'i*), thus synchronizing with the third, which represents it as mixed. In this way the controversy over the goodness or evil of human nature was settled.

In Chu Hsi's system, nature is different from mind. In the *Yü Lei* (5), two passages illustrate this difference:

> Question: "Is [man's] intellectual faculty the mind or the nature?"
> Answer: "The intellectual faculty is the mind alone and not the nature. For the nature is nothing but the *Li*."
> Another passage reads:
> Question: "As regards consciousness, is it the mind's intellectual faculty that is thus conscious, or is it the product of the *Ch'i*?"
> Answer: "It is not the *Ch'i* alone. There is first the *Li* of consciousness; but this *Li* by itself cannot exercise consciousness. There can be consciousness only when the *Ch'i* has condensed to form physical shapes, and the *Li* has combined with the *Ch'i*. This is similar to the flame of this candle. It is because of the rich fat that we have so much light."

Thus the mind, like all other things, embodies the *Li* with the *Ch'i*. The difference between the mind and the nature is that the mind is concrete and the nature is abstract. Hence the mind can have activities, such as thinking and feeling, but the nature cannot. Then Chu Hsi, on the basis of this difference, went further to discuss the relationship between the mind, human nature, feelings and capacity. In the *Yü Lei*, one passage (5) reads:

> The nature is the *Li* of the mind; the feelings are the movements of the mind; capacity is that by which the feelings can act in a certain way. The feelings and capacity are in fact very close to each other. But the feelings are aroused by [the affection of] external things, and their courses [of action] curve and twist in various ways. Likewise, capacity acts in the same way. No matter how much they are complicated and diversified, they all invariably emanate from the mind.

To illustrate this relationship, let us quote another passage from the same place:

> The mind may be likened to water, and the nature is the *Li* of that water. The nature represents the water when it is still, whereas the feelings represent the water when it is in movement. Desire is the pouring forth of the water until it overflows, and capacity is the strength of the water which enables it thus to pour forth. That its pouring forth may be rapid or slow depends upon the differences of its capacity. This is what Yi-ch'uan [Ch'eng I] means when he says that the nature is endowed by Heaven, whereas capacity is endowed by the *Ch'i*. The nature alone remains constant, whereas the feelings, the mind and capacity all conform to the *Ch'i*.

As noted above, the *Li* of all men is the same, but unfortunately their *Ch'i* is not. It is, according to Chu Hsi, the *Ch'i* in its purity or impurity that makes men different. The problem of self-cultivation, therefore, is how to remove the impurity of the *Ch'i* in order to recapture one's original nature. According to Chu Hsi, all one's efforts needed in the process of self-cultivation must be concentrated on what Ch'eng I called the "exercise of seriousness" and the *chih chih* (extension of knowledge). As pointed out by Chu Hsi, the "exercise of seriousness" simply means that one should realize the existence within oneself of a "luminous spiritual something" which should be carefully guarded from the impediment of murky desires (the impure *Ch'i*). Of the obscuring of one's true nature, Chu Hsi said: "If one could only realize that it is one's desire that thus causes this obscuring, then one would be enlightened" (*Yü Lei*, 12).

As for the "extension of knowledge," Chu Hsi, like Ch'eng I, based his idea of self-cultivation on the passage from the opening section of the *Ta Hsüeh*, previously quoted (Chapter 5), in which it is stated that "extension of knowledge depends upon the investigation of things" (*ko wu*). Chu Hsi's interpretation of this statement is found in the following passage:

> The statement, "the extension of knowledge depends upon the investigation of things," means that if we extend our knowledge, we must consider things and gain exhaustive knowledge of their *Li*. This is because there is no intelligence in men's minds without knowledge, and there is no single thing in the world without the *Li*. But if the *Li* is not exhaustively studied, this knowledge will be limited in its extension. Hence the teaching of the *Ta Hsüeh* must at its outset lead students to study all things in the world, proceeding from what is already known of the *Li* in these things, to gain a further exhaustive knowledge of it until the limit is reached. After such efforts are put forth for a considerable time, one will become in a moment of sudden illumination completely enlightened. Then in all things, whether the internal or the external, the essence or the husk, there will be nothing which is not comprehended, and the mind in its substance and function will become enlightened. This is what is meant by "investigation of things" (*ko wu*). This is what is meant by the "extension of knowledge" (*chih chih*). (*Ta Hsüeh Chang-chü*, or *Commentary on the Great Learning*, Section on *Ko Wu*.)

This interpretation of Chu Hsi was evidently based on the views of Ch'eng I. Following Ch'eng I, Chu Hsi laid great stress on "the extension of knowledge" as the means of attaining moral cultivation and regarded the knowledge here referred to as a knowledge of the *Li*. According to the Ch'eng-Chu system, such knowledge can be best gained by the exhaustive study of the *Li*, and acquisition of such knowledge, if sufficiently sustained, will eventually lead to a moment of sudden enlightenment. This interpretation, which combines knowledge and moral cultivation into a unity, did not satisfy all the Neo-Confucian scholars, and one of the most prominent advocates of a different interpretation was the philosopher Wang Yang-ming, whose view will be considered later.

Idealistic Neo-Confucianism

The system of Chu Hsi, based as he admitted on the ideas of Ch'eng I, became the orthodox Confucian view, but it did not immediately win the unqualified acceptance of the majority of Confucian scholars. Chu Hsi entered into controversy with several rival interpreters of Confucianism whom he deemed heterodox. His greatest rival was Lu Hsiang-shan (also known as Lu Chiu-yüan), the leading spirit in the *Hsin-Hsüeh* school of Neo-Confucianism, which was further developed in the fifteenth century by Wang Yang-ming.

The fundamental differences between Lu Hsiang-shan and Chu Hsi might be simply stated thus: (1) To Chu Hsi, "the nature is *Li*"; to Lu Hsiang-shan, "the mind is *Li*." (2) For Chu Hsi, "the investigation of things" is the key to knowledge as the means of attaining spiritual cultivation; for Lu Hsiang-shan, the cultivation is to be attained chiefly through meditation, intuition and sudden enlightenment. The point at issue is that Lu Hsiang-shan, as an idealist, attached much importance to the mind, but denied the distinction between the mind and the nature, as maintained by Chu Hsi. In other words, Lu Hsiang-shan believed in the existence of one world (the mind) instead of the two of Chu Hsi (the metaphysical and the physical). Thus Lu Hsiang-shan said:

All men have the mind; all minds are endowed with the *Li*. The mind is the *Li* (The *Complete Works*, XI). The mind is one and the *Li* is one. Perfect truth is reduced to unity; the essential principle is never a duality. The mind and the *Li* can never be separated into two (*Ibid.*, I).

Moreover, Lu Hsiang-shan believed that a person's mind is fundamentally one with the universe, but unfortunately, this oneness is often obscured or beclouded either by "selfish desires" or by "dogmatic views." Hence he maintained that, in order to attain moral cultivation, one needs first of all to cherish the mind, which is originally good; or, as it is sometimes expressed, "to establish what is most important." Like Chu Hsi, Lu Hsiang-shan believed that one's mind could be restored to its innate goodness, but he disagreed with Chu Hsi as to the techniques for restoring the "original mind." As noted above, Chu Hsi's method consists in "seeking knowledge by investigating things." Lu Hsiang-shan, however, regarded this method as one of complication and futility, and so he advocated a simpler and easier method of cultivation which consists in "following what is natural to one's mind." Here is Lu Hsiang-shan's advice:

> Concentrate your spirit. Be your own master. "All things are already complete in oneself." What is it that is deficient? When I should be compassionate, I shall naturally display compassion; when I should be ashamed and disgusted, I shall naturally display shame and disgust; when I should be generous, lenient, affectionate, and tender, I shall naturally display generosity, leniency, affection and tenderness; when I should be strong and firm, I shall naturally display strength and firmness (*Complete Works*, 35).

Lu Hsiang-shan agreed with Mencius that man is self-sufficient if only he submits himself to the mind, which, even when obscured by human desires, is fundamentally as perfect as ever. Therefore, what man should do is to seek what is in himself. There is, as he asserted, no need to seek knowledge from the outside, for the real knowledge is in our mind; thus his oft quoted words: "What kind of book did Yao and Shun [the legendary Sage-Rulers] study?" The meaning is that the ancient sage-rulers cultivated themselves without having books to read. Hence it is in our mind, not in the external world, not in books about it either, that we can seek for real knowledge. Everything else is trivial information. "In learning a man should first comprehend what is fundamental" (*Complete Works*, 34). Once a man had grasped the "fundamental," Lu Hsiang-shan asserted, "all the Six Classics would serve only as his footnotes" (*Ibid.*). Here we can see how Lu Hsiang-shan deviated from Chu Hsi in his philosophy and method of spiritual cultivation. Because he attached primary importance to the "original mind" and the rejection of knowledge-seeking, Lu Hsiang-shan has been accused of being a *Ch'an* Buddhist. In fairness we must concede that basically Lu Hsiang-shan was a Confucianist in his views. Although he applied the technique of the *Ch'an* school for moral cultivation, he forsook its negative and escapist attitude toward life and criticized the Buddhist idea of withdrawing from the world as "selfish and calculated." [2]

Since 1313 Chu Hsi's interpretation of Confucianism had been accepted as orthodoxy and made the basis of the state examinations. By the late fifteenth century many Confucian scholars, however, became restive under Chu Hsi's orthodoxy and wished to think for themselves. The most outstanding philosopher was Wang Yang-ming (also known as Wang Shou-jen), who continued and developed the philosophy of the *Hsin Hsüeh* school in opposition to that of the *Li Hsüeh* school.

Wang Yang-ming was not merely a distinguished philosopher, but also a remarkable general and statesman. He held various important offices, but his real greatness lay in his originality in working out a philosophy which stemmed from Lu Hsiang-shan. In his youthful years, he seems to have studied both Taoism and Buddhism, but he ended by clinging to Confucianism. At first he was an ardent student of the Ch'eng-Chu school, which, it will be recalled, had professed to advocate the search for *Li* through the "investigation of things." By an experience of sudden illumination after a long period of "investigating things" as the sole means of moral perfection, as advocated by Chu Hsi, he announced a principle of his own, called *liang chih* (intuitive knowledge).

Wang Yang-ming claimed to be Lu Hsiang-shan's legitimate successor. Certainly his affinity to the latter may be found in his preface to Lu Hsiang-shan's *Complete Works* (7):

> The study of sagehood is the study of mind. . . . When the mind and the *Li* are separated, the effort toward proficiency and unity is lost. Then many scholars have eschewed the orthodox doctrine and become interested in the pursuit of such inessentials as knowledge, terms, numbers, and institutions. That was how the so-called "investigation of things" originated. What such scholars do not know is that the mind is *Li* and that neither the mind nor the *Li* can be found in the external world . . . In the Sung period, Chou [Tun-i] and the Ch'eng brothers traced their thought back to the orthodoxy of Confucius and Mencius. . . . Since then, the tradition of proficiency and unity has been restored. Then Lu Hsiang-shan was born in the Southern Sung period. Though his character with respect to mental calmness was not equal to that of Chou or either of the Ch'eng brothers, yet the simplicity and directness of his method made him a successor of Mencius. His daring arguments were the result of his temperament, but his belief in the supremacy of the mind was identical with that of Mencius. Therefore, I say: "The philosophy of Lu Hsiang-shan is the philosophy of Mencius."

Here we can see how much he admired the philosophy of Lu Hsiang-shan. This is why Wang Yang-ming is often mentioned together with Lu Hsiang-shan as a founder of the Neo-Confucian school of Idealism (*Hsin Hsüeh*), also called the Lu-Wang school, which elicited a wide response from scholars in the late Ming period. Among his writings there are two important treatises: *Ta Hsüeh Wen (Dialogue on the Great*

Learning) and *Ch'uan-hsi lu* (*Record of Instructions*) in which his dynamic idealism is well illustrated. These two treatises are now contained in *Wang Wen-ch'eng Kung Ch'uen-shu* (*Complete Works of Wang Yang-ming*).

As regards his philosophy, Wang Yang-ming agreed with Lu Hsiang-shan that "the mind itself is *Li*." Wang strongly believed that unless there is mind there will be no *Li*. Thus he said:

> The mind itself is *Li*. So in the world can there yet be any thing or any *Li* outside of the mind? (*Ch'uan-hsi lu*).

And again:

> The substance of the mind is the nature, and the nature is the *Li*. Therefore, since there is the mind of filial piety, it follows that there is the *Li* of filial piety. If there were no such a mind, there would be no such *Li*. And since there is the mind of loyalty to the sovereign, it follows that there is the *Li* of loyalty. If there were no such mind, there would be no such *Li*. How can the *Li* be outside of the mind? (*Ibid.*).

Wang Yang-ming said further:

> The mind, if not obstructed by selfish desires, is *T'ien Li* (Heavenly Principle), which requires nothing added from the outside. When this mind, which has become completely identical with *T'ien Li*, arises to serve parents, there is filial piety; when it arises to serve the sovereign, there is loyalty; when it arises to deal with friends and to govern the people, there are faithfulness and *jen*. What is important for the mind is to make the effort to remove human desires and to preserve the *T'ien Li* (*Ibid.*).

Here lies the essence of Wang Yang-ming's philosophy. It is that the mind is the supreme legislator as well as the embodiment of the *Li*. All we need to do is to follow the dictates of the mind, that is "the intuitive knowledge" (*liang chih*) of the mind. *Liang chih* is a term taken from a passage about the "four beginnings" in the *Meng Tzu* and is similar in conception to the "original mind" of Lu Hsiang-shan. The intuitive knowledge of which Wang Yang-ming spoke is nothing mysterious. It is just natural feeling. Thus he said:

> This intuitive knowledge is just what Mencius meant when he said: "The sense of right and wrong is common to all men" [The *Meng Tzu* IA–6]. The sense of right and wrong requires no deliberation to know, nor does it rely on learning to function. This is why it is called intuitive knowledge. It is my nature endowed by Heaven, the original substance of my mind, naturally intelligent, shining, clear, and conscious (*Ta Hsüeh Wen*).

Hence Wang Yang-ming maintained that "knowing is the original substance of the mind." Here the word "knowing" stands for "intuitive knowledge." According to Wang Yang-ming, the first response in our mind to the external things is always the manifestation of the original good, the intuitive knowledge. This is exactly what he meant when he said in the *Ta Hsüeh Wen*: "The original substance of the illustrious virtue is what is known as the intuitive knowledge." The common illustration he and his followers used is that when a man sees a child about to fall into a well, his first response is the feeling of alarm and trying to save the child from falling. Other ideas, such as to show his bravery, to make friendship with the parents of the child, come to the mind only afterwards. The first is the response of intuitive knowledge, the others are calculated and selfish. This intuitive knowledge, as Wang Yang-ming asserted, is shared by all men, the only difference being that whereas the great man who "regards Heaven and Earth and the myriad things as one body," preserves it intact, in its original state, the small men, who "make cleavage between the self and others," have been led astray by external things, so that their intuitive knowledge is contaminated by selfish desires. Therefore, there is the necessity for moral cultivation to recover the lost intuitive knowledge. According to Wang

Yang-ming, the moral cultivation needed is that which in the *Ta Hsüeh* is described as *Ko wu chih chih,* interpreted by Chu Hsi, we may recall, as meaning "the investigation of things and the extension of knowledge." But Wang Yang-ming advocated quite a different interpretation of this phrase. Concerning *chih chih* (investigation of knowledge) he said in the *Ta Hsüeh Wen*:

> In the *I Ching*, it is said: "Knowing the utmost, one should reach it" [Commentary on the Hexagram *Ch'ien*]. "Knowing the utmost" means knowledge and "reaching it" means extension. Hence "the extension of knowledge" is not what later scholars [Chu Hsi and his group] understand as enriching and widening knowledge. It is simply extending the intuitive knowledge of our mind.

From this viewpoint, he further interpreted "the extension of intuitive knowledge" as not "something illusory, hazy, in a vacuum [devoid of the *Li*], and unreal"; it is rather "something real." (*Ibid.*) "Therefore," he concluded, "the extension of knowledge (*chih chih*) must consist in the investigation of things (*ko wu*). As for the meaning of "*ko wu*" (investigation of things), he said further:

> [The word] *wu* (things) means "affairs." For the expression of an idea (*yi*), there must be an affair. The affair toward which the idea is directed is called "a thing" (*wu*). [The word] *ko* [used in the phrase "*ko wu,*" "investigation of things] means *cheng* [rectifying]. It means to rectify what is unrectified in order to restore it to a state of rectitude. To rectify what is unrectified means to get rid of the evil. To restore it to rectitude means to practice goodness" (*Ibid.*).

This interpretation indeed was a great departure from what Chu Hsi meant when he said: "The statement 'the extension of knowledge (*chih chih*) lies in the investigation of things (*ko wu*)' means that we should apply ourselves to [the study of] things (*wu*) so as to gain an exhaustive knowledge of their *Li*" (Chu Hsi's *Ta Hsüeh Chang-chü*).

It is obvious that the central thesis of Wang Yang-ming's philosophy is to be based on "the extension of intuitive knowledge." Such a theory was indeed simple and direct, and its interpretation of the term "*ko wu*" as "to rectify the mind" [3] is certainly incompatible with Chu Hsi's theory of "investigating into the *Li* in everything for the purpose of extending one's knowledge to the utmost." In short, the controversy between the great Neo-Confucian philosophers may be said to center around the question of whether the term "*ko wu*" should be interpreted as "to investigate things" or as "to rectify the mind"—that is, the issue between objective study and intuitive knowledge.

Finally, some consideration must be given to Wang Yang-ming's doctrine of the "unity of knowledge and practice." The relation between knowledge and practice was constantly debated among Confucian scholars. That action is related to knowledge, they all agreed. On this subject, the Neo-Confucian philosophers, as noted above, laid stress not only on the "exhaustive study of the *Li*," but also on the "deliberate exercise of seriousness." Clearly, they recognized the mutual relation and equal importance of knowledge and practice, but not their unity. Chu Hsi came nearer to that when he said:

> Knowledge and practice mutually involve each other. Their mutual relation can be compared to that of eyes and legs. For without legs one cannot walk, and without eyes one cannot see. In point of priority, knowledge precedes practice; in point of importance, practice predominates over knowledge (*Complete Works*, 3).

Chu Hsi placed his emphasis on action. Wang Yang-ming was indeed the first who distinctly advocated the doctrine of the unity of knowledge and practice, as elaborated in the following dialogue reported in *Ch'uan-hsi lu.*

Hsü Ai [Wang's student] said: "For example, people to-day who know that filial piety should be due to parents, and fraternal love to brothers, fail to put either into practice. This means that knowledge and action are two separate things."

The Teacher [Wang] said: "This is the outcome of the separation [of knowledge and action] caused by selfish desires, and is not in accordance with the original substance of knowledge and action. There has never been a man who knew and yet did not act. To know and fail to act is equivalent to not knowing. The sages and worthies taught men both knowledge and action, precisely because they wished them to restore the original substance, and not merely to act in the manner you have just indicated.

To illustrate his theory, Wang Yang-ming said further:

Seeing beauty is a matter of knowledge, whereas loving the beautiful means action. And yet, as soon as one sees beauty one loves it; one does not first see it and then make up his mind to love it. Similarly, smelling an evil odor pertains to knowledge, while disliking it is action. Yet as soon as one smells an evil odor, he dislikes it; one does not smell it first and then make up his mind to dislike it. But a man with his nostrils stuffed may not smell the malodorous object before him, and so he may not even dislike it. In this case, he does not know that it is actually evil-smelling. No one can properly be said to know filial piety and fraternal love unless he actually practices them. Merely being able to talk about these virtues does not mean knowing them.

Then Wang Yang-ming summed up his theory:

I have said that knowledge motivates action, and that practice implies the execution of knowledge. Knowing is the beginning of action, and doing is the completion of knowledge. When this is understood, though one speaks only of knowing, the doing is already included; likewise, though one may speak only of action, the knowing is also implied.

In his idealistic system of thought, Wang Yang-ming did display some resemblance to *Ch'an* Buddhism. Consciously or unconsciously he seems to have been influenced by Buddhist ideology. However, he was not a Buddhist thinker; he was a Confucian philosopher. There is nothing in him of the ascetic and pessimistic outlook on life characteristic of Buddhism. Moreover, his profound respect for antiquity, his keen interest in current problems, his special emphasis on action make him a genuine humanist. Wang Yang-ming was in fact a man of action, not only preaching it but also practising himself what he taught. His intuitive idealism has had a far greater influence on modern China than the speculative rationalism of Chu Hsi. It was this emphasis on action which motivated K'ang Yu-wei (1858–1927) to provide Confucian justification for his famous reform movement of 1898. It has been surmised that even "today the Chinese Communists' concern for a Marxist 'unity of theory and practice' . . . can make use of Wang Yang-ming's terminology." [4] The modern trend in Confucianism will be discussed in the next chapter.

CHAPTER 9

Confucianism in Modern China

During the last four hundred years, two major intellectual forces have arisen to play important roles in the development of Chinese thought and particularly of Confucianism, namely, the revolt against Neo-Confucianism and the impact of the West. As noted in the preceding chapter, Confucian orthodoxy was firmly established when Chu Hsi's interpretation was officially approved as the basis for the civil service examinations. This orthodoxy soon lost much of its vigor and hardened into dogma. Meanwhile, the government examination, which had become rigid and formalized, stressed the memorizing of Confucian classics and the writing of stylized essays at the expense of the true spirit of Confucianism. It was only natural, then, that during the Ching dynasty (1644–1911), an independent group of scholars arose and launched an attack on the Neo-Confucianism of the Sung and Ming periods, which, they claimed, had been corrupted by Buddhist and Taoist ideologies. In protest, they styled themselves "followers of the Han Learning (*Han Hsüeh*)" to show that they sought to liberate the Chinese mind from the shackles of "Sung Learning (*Sung Hsüeh*)" by going back to the Confucianism of the Han and pre-Han periods. Since then, the controversy between Ch'ing scholars of the Han Learning and Sung Learning has been one of the greatest in the history of Chinese thought.

The Ch'ing scholars distinguished themselves for their skepticism and criticism on the basis of what they called the method of "empirical research" (*k'ao-chü* or *k'ao-cheng*, literally, "search for evidence"). Their real significance lies in their effort to authenticate and correct the numerous texts of the Confucian school as well as those of the other schools. It is mainly due to their labors that these ancient texts are now more readable and intelligible than they had ever been before. But, unfortunately, they devoted themselves to linguistic studies and textual criticism, and neglected philosophical studies.

In the meantime, there was another group of Ch'ing scholars, who stressed practicality of thought, and exerted a great influence on the modern trends of Chinese thinking. The men of this group were scornful of mere book-learning and metaphysical speculation. Their academic effort was not just to expound abstract doctrines based on "the true teachings of Confucius and Mencius"; they pushed their researches into the political, social and economic realms as well. And while they failed to develop a strong movement, their stress on actual experience and practical problems did much to bring about a new philosophical impulse, under the influence of which the Chinese are still living.

With foreign wars and internal rebellions in the middle of the nineteenth century, this academic activity declined. The Han Learning was not forgotten, however, and, under the impact of the West, gave rise to the intellectual revolution which rocked the last years of the nineteenth century and the early twentieth century.

K'ang Yu-wei and Confucian Church

The Ch'ing reaction against the Neo-Confucianism took a new turn by the end of the nineteenth century. In Chapter 6, we noted that the Han scholars divided themselves into two groups: the New-Script school and the Old-Script school. The Han Learning, during the early Ch'ing period, was in substance that of the Old-Script school. But at the end of the nineteenth century and early in the twentieth century there were new intellectuals who discriminated against the "spurious" classics of the Old-Script school in favor of the "authentic" ones of the New-Script school. On the basis of the *Kung-yang* doctrine of *Ch'un-ch'iu*, as advocated by Tung Chung-shu, they believed that Confucius formulated new laws and devised new institutions for all ages to come and thus made himself a "new king and founder of religion." The leader of this movement was K'ang Yu-wei (1858–1927), the last of the great traditional Confucian scholars. Let us see how K'ang Yu-wei tried to transform Confucianism from a moral philosophy into a religion. His was not the first attempt to do this but it was perhaps the most notable.

K'ang Yu-wei was brought up in an old Confucian family. His great grandfather, K'ang Shih-p'an, was a private tutor in Confucian classics and a dedicated Confucian scholar. His grandfather, K'ang Tsan-hsiu, was the superintendent of education in Lienchow district, a man who devoted himself to the study of the Neo-Confucianism of the Sung dynasty.

When K'ang Yu-wei was only eleven years of age his father died and he was sent to Lienchow to study with his grandfather. In 1876 K'ang began a new education under the great scholar of Kwangtung, Chu Tzu-ch'i (1807–1881). K'ang studied under Chu for about three years, from 1876 to 1878, and then, in the autumn and winter months of 1878, K'ang faced a mental crisis. He wrote:

> I felt that in burying myself daily in heaps of waste papers I was smothering my intellectual faculties. I became increasingly bored and disliked doing my studies. Suddenly, I stopped doing them and threw away all books. Shutting the door and refusing to associate with my friends, I sat in quietude to cultivate my mind. My behavior was regarded by my fellow students as extremely strange.

> One day, when I sat in meditation, I perceived suddenly that I was in an all-pervading unity with Heaven, Earth, and all things and that light shone forth in great profusion. Regarding myself as a Sage, I smiled with happiness. But thinking of the sufferings of mankind, I suddenly wept in sorrow.
>
> Winter arrived and I took leave of Master Chiu-chiang, having decided to return home and practice quiet meditation.[1]

This crisis brought to an end K'ang's association with Chu, but it was a turning point in his intellectual career. It marked a religious beginning for him and he "departed from the traditional classics" and turned to the study of Buddhism and Christianity. K'ang did not renounce Confucianism as taught by his teacher Chu Tzu-ch'i. Instead, his revelation widened his intellectual vista by liberating his mind from the shackles of Neo-Confucianism so that he might lay the foundations of his syncretic thought and yet remain essentially Confucian. He had "got religion." But he was a Confucian. He would make Confucianism a religion.

The study of Buddhist texts and Christian and other books from the West helped K'ang in the early 1880's to transcend traditional Confucianism and to see the classics in a new light. He broke away from Neo-Confucian tradition built on the Rationalism (*Li-hsüeh*) of Chu Hsi (1130–1200) and became interested solely in practical studies. K'ang also immersed himself in various works on history, political institutions, geography, mathematics, geometry and sciences, in all of which he hoped to gain profound insight into the mysteries of the universe and human life, not merely information but inspiration.

It must be remembered that during the nineteenth century the traditional order in China disintegrated rapidly. The unequal treaties forced upon China after the Opium War of 1839–1842 gave foreigners a privileged position in China and a strong hold upon its economic life. Resident aliens and corporations enjoyed extraterritorial status exempting them from Chinese law and authority. Under the Inland Navigation Regulations of 1898, for example, foreigners could travel freely along a sea coast of 5,000 nautical miles. Moreover, foreign goods, again under the protection of the unequal treaties, were dumped on the Chinese market, and native products could not successfully compete with them. In the course of a few decades, China became in effect a tributary state to foreign powers.

Besides Western encroachments, the Manchu government faced growing unrest among the Chinese people. After the Opium War there were six serious internal revolutions: one in the south by the Taipings (1850–1864), one in the north by the Niens (1855–1868), and four by Moslems in the northwest and southwest (1855–1872, 1862–1873) and in central Asia (1862–1876, 1866–1878). China was in chaos.

The revolutions were crushed one by one by the might of imperial armies, but millions of people lost their lives and the rural communities were deeply affected. As a result, despite the desperate effort by the Manchu government to tighten its control, there was inevitably a decline of imperial rule both at home and abroad.

The worsening conditions of the Empire convinced K'ang Yu-wei that only extensive and timely reform could save China from dismemberment at the hands of Western powers. Politically K'ang's reform movement was a failure, but culturally and religiously K'ang did much to stimulate the thinking of the Chinese people and to teach them a critical attitude toward the Confucian classics.

The significance of K'ang Yu-wei as a thinker lies in his attempt to provide a Confucian justification for his basic ideas of reform. He wrote many commentaries on the Confucian classics and read his new ideas into them. Before 1894, K'ang wrote two outstanding books, one entitled *Hsin-hsüeh wei-ching k'ao* (*The Forged Classics of the Hsin Dynasty*) and the other *K'ung-tzu kai-chih k'ao* (*Confucius as a Reformer*).

In the first book he charged that the so-called Confucian classics of the Old-Script school, which were defended by Liu Hsin, one of the most remarkable scholars of the Han period, were forgeries, while the books of the New-Script school, headed by Tung Chung-shu, the greatest of the early Han scholars, were the really authentic texts.

K'ang Yu-wei, as a Confucian scholar of the Kung-yang school, attempted to break down the prestige of the popular Han school interpretation of Confucian classics which was generally accepted at that time and to open a whole new realm of thought. This new interpretation did indeed create a great turmoil in scholarly circles. His enemies, especially those who opposed the reform movement, threw K'ang out of the Confucian school. For example, Yeh Te-hui (1864–1927) wrote that in attempting to overthrow the accepted Confucian tradition, K'ang revealed himself as "barbarian at heart," thinly disguised by the "Confucian countenance" which he assumed. It was ironic that the man who was attempting to give the Chinese intellectual weapons against the "barbarians" should be accused of being one of them.

That did not stop K'ang. In fact, he wrote his second book in 1896 and published it just a few months before the fateful "One Hundred-Days' Reform." He further demonstrated that Confucius was not merely a transmitter of historical tradition but also a creator of a "teaching" which encompassed all enduring truths.

Moreover, according to K'ang Yu-wei, the greatness of Confucius lies in his having written all the Six Classics—the *I* (Change), the *Shih* (Poetry), the *Shu* (History), the *Li* (Rites), the *Yueh* (Music) and the *Ch'un Ch'iu* (Spring and Autumn Annals)—to promote reform in his own time. K'ang further maintained that "only when a scholar recognizes that the Six Classics were written by Confucius can he understand why Confucius was the great sage, the founder of the doctrine, and the model for all ages; and why Confucius alone was called the Great Master."

Meanwhile, K'ang was very much impressed by the works of Christian missionaries, particularly the English and American Protestants. What the missionaries said and did shaped, in some degree, the ideas K'ang held concerning the West. We can see at this distance that Christian missonaries in China had hardly any effect at all on that vast people, but their influence on K'ang himself was great.

Moreover, in the 1860's the Protestant missionary scholars took the lead with the assistance of Chinese associates in publishing Chinese translations and digests of Western books on history, literature and science. For example, among the British contributing to the cultural introduction were William Muirhead (1822–1887), Joseph Edkins (1823–1905), Alexander Wylie (1815–1887), James Legge (1815–1897), who became a great Sinologist and translated the Confucian classics into English, and Timothy Richard (1845–1919) who edited a Chinese daily newspaper at Tientsin. During the brief period of reform in China, Timothy Richard became a foreign advisor to the Emperor. Some of the Americans included W.A.P. Martin, who was president of a language school (Tung-wen Kuan), Samuel Wells Williams, Young J. Allen and John Fryer.

Because of the influence of these missionaries, K'ang in the summer of 1898 formally proposed that Confucianism be established as the "state religion" and a Confucian "church" be instituted. K'ang's insistence on establishing Confucianism as a "state religion" was in all probability prompted by what he had learned of Western religious practices. In fact, K'ang regarded himself much in the same light as Martin Luther and the leaders of the Reformation.

In terms of principles and philosophy, K'ang Yu-wei perceived the similarity between the Christian doctrine of love and the Confucian doctrine of *jen*. However, K'ang was opposed to the adoption of the Christian religion by the Chinese. According to K'ang, there is a basic difference between Christianity and Confucianism.

Confucianism may not be devoid of religious implications, but K'ang argued that Confucianism is essentially secular and superior to Christianity because Confucius "swept away divine authority." K'ang maintained that "living in the environment of perfected social institutions will enable men to cultivate their basically good nature, and to perfect it." In fact, what K'ang really wanted was not a "city of God" in Heaven, but a "Kingdom of Man" on earth. Confucianism, established as a state church, was his answer to the problem.

K'ang was impressed by the example of Christianity as a state religion in many Western countries; he and some of his disciples in the early days of the new Republic clamoured vociferously and made Confucian orthodoxy the national religion of the Chinese people. After the overthrow of the Manchu dynasty and the establishment of the Republic in 1911 K'ang braced himself for a great campaign to propagate Confucius' teachings. He and his followers formed Confucian associations for the study and exaltation of the Sage's teachings. When the Constitutional Convention met in 1915, K'ang Yu-wei again proposed that a clause be included in the new constitution to establish Confucianism as a state religion and to institute a Confucian "church" for the new Republic.

The uproar that followed this proposal was terrific; he met head on with a strong opposition from the members of Catholic, Protestant, Moslem, Buddhist and Taoist organizations. These religious organizations formed a "Society for Religious Freedom" to block K'ang Yu-wei's state-religion movement. Consequently, after much squabbling and name-calling, the Draft Convention adopted a compromise resolution endorsing the moral superiority of Confucian teaching, but not hailing it a national religion.

The Constitution, anyway, was never adopted and, when it was finally scrapped, gone with it was the last hope of K'ang Yu-wei. His abortive attempt at deifying Confucius, therefore, indicated only his desperate plight at the dawn of a new era.

The Ta-t'ung: A World Utopia

More significant than his attempts at reconstructing Confucianism is K'ang Yu-wei's conception of a new world Utopia. This he called *Ta T'ung*. The two characters *Ta* and *T'ung* are a phrase in the section *Li Yün* (The Evolution of *Li*) in the *Li Chi,* denoting the glorious consummation of world peace and world unity.

In more concrete terms, the *Ta-t'ung* philosophy of K'ang Yu-wei consists of the principles of universal love and equality: "The *Tao* of *Ta-t'ung* is the acme of fairness, justice, love, and good government," whereby will be realized the principles of universal love and equality, happiness and justice for all.

Specifically speaking, the principle of universal love is the foundation of *Ta-t'ung,* while that of equality is the function of *Ta-t'ung.* In other words, the principle of universal love is the motive or purpose of *Ta-t'ung,* while that of equality is the result or end of *Ta-t'ung.* Hence, K'ang Yu-wei wrote: "After mankind has become equal, great *jen* will abound." Though these two principles are complementary to each other, yet the *Ta-t'ung* centers in the principle of universal love.

In the mind of K'ang Yu-wei, love, as the "constituent principle of life," had a universal penetration like that of ether or electricity. When this principle of universal love is realized on earth, the perfect unity of the world will be assured. Then all the distinctions and inequality of nations, of classes, and of sexes will be eliminated.

Because of the principles of universal love and equality, it is necessary to put the *Ta-t'ung* into practice. K'ang Yu-wei then made a very detailed study of the world as it was and developed his scheme for union with logical consistency. He borrowed the theory of historical progress based upon the concept of the Three Ages, as found in the *Kung-yang Chuan (Commentary on the Ch'un Ch'iu),* the *Li Yün* section of the *Li Chi,* and illustrated by the Han scholars Tung Chung-shu and Ho Hsiu (129–182).

As we noted before when mentioning this theory, there were Three Ages: the Age of Disorder, the Age of Approaching Peace, and the Age of Great Peace. In the Age of Disorder, Confucius devoted himself to his own state of Lu and took Lu as the center of his reforms. In the Age of Approaching Peace, having given good government to his own state, Confucius took China as the center of his reforms so as to bring peace and good order to other states. And in the Age of Great Peace, Confucius finally took the world as the center of his reforms in order to civilize all the surrounding barbarians and unite humanity into one harmonious whole. Believing that Confucius was a teacher with divine personality, K'ang Yu-wei now revived this theory. He said, in his famous book *Ta T'ung Shu*, written in 1884:

> Having long considered [the problems of attaining happiness and doing away with suffering] and grieved over it, the sage-king Confucius, with divine enlightenment, set up the law of Three Systems [represented by three institutional patterns: the "Red," "White" and "Black"] and the Three Ages: following [the Age of] Disorder, [the world] will change to the Ages of Approaching Peace and Great Peace; that is, following [the Age of] Small Tranquility, [the world] will advance to [the Age of] *Ta-t'ung*.[2]

K'ang Yu-wei further maintained that the growing communications between East and West, and the political and social reforms in Europe and America, showed that the world is evolving from the Age of Disorder toward the Age of Approaching Peace. And this in turn will be followed by the Age of Great Peace, the last stage of human progress, in which "there will be unity of the world irrespective of the size of countries and distance between them; with the national states abolished, and racial distinctions eliminated, and traditions and cultures all in harmony, there will be one world of peace and happiness." Then K'ang Yu-wei added, "Confucius had long known all this in advance." Confucius, he said, was the prophet of One World.

In accordance with the process of evolution, K'ang Yu-wei asserted, the principle of universal love was to be widened progressively as the world advanced from a lower stage of development to a higher level. Thus in the Age of Disorder priority was given to members of one's family but "in the Age of Great Peace all will be treated in one same way." In place of the differentiated loyalties which bound men to their particular social groups in the Age of Disorder, there would be in the Age of Great Peace only an undifferentiated feeling of love, which K'ang had identified with the Confucian virtue of *jen*.

However, the principle of universal love, as the controlling element in human relations in general, does not exactly coincide with the original concept of *jen* as developed by Confucius and Mencius. K'ang's views on this are rather similar to those of the Western utilitarians.

K'ang presented a psychological argument: "Now, the consciousness possessed by living creatures derives from the fact that their brains contain *ling* [*anima* or intellect]. The contact [of the brain] with material and immaterial [objects] results in what seems to be either appropriate or inappropriate, suitable or unsuitable. What is suitable and appropriate to the brain is taken by the soul to be pleasure, while what is unsuitable and inappropriate is taken by the soul to be pain."

Then K'ang Yu-wei reinforced his argument with analysis of the laws and institutions of history, to show that they were all established with the purpose of enabling one to attain happiness (pleasure) and avoid suffering (pain). K'ang Yu-wei emphasized that all living creatures were governed by pleasure and pain. Hence, he wrote: "the establishment of laws and creation of teachings which will cause men to enjoy only pleasure and no pain is the goodness of all goodness . . . and that which causes men to have much pain and little pleasure is the negation of goodness." Acceptance of this criterion means that the laws and teachings of "the *Tao* of *Ta-t'ung*" must necessarily conform to those enabling mankind to attain happiness and avoid suffering.

According to K'ang's analysis, the sources of all human suffering can be traced to "nine boundaries." The first is called nation-boundary: division by territorial frontiers and by tribes. The second is called class-boundary: division by noble and base; by pure and impure. The third is called race-boundary: division by yellow, white, brown and black. The fourth is called sex-boundary: division by male and female. The fifth is called family-boundary: private relationships between father and son, husband and wife, elder and younger brothers and sisters. The sixth is called occupation-boundary: the private ownership of agriculture, industry and commerce. The seventh is called disorder-boundary: the existence of unequal, unthorough, dissimilar and unjust laws. The eighth is called kind-boundary: the distinction between human beings, birds, beasts, fish and insects. The ninth is called suffering-boundary: by suffering, giving rise to suffering; its perpetuation is inexhaustible and endless, beyond conception.

These nine boundaries are the sources of all suffering and therefore K'ang's scheme for attaining the global utopia calls for the abolition of these nine boundaries. With them gone, there will only be One World under the principle of *Ta-t'ung*, where we shall enjoy long life and eternal enlightenment.

K'ang Yu-wei spoke with confidence that this global utopia would be realized inevitably within two or three hundred years. He outlined a complete system for a universal parliament and an elaborate universal government; he also worked out a long chart of the Three Ages in the evolution of uniting various nations into One World.

Once the world government of *Ta-t'ung* had been firmly established, K'ang Yu-wei would proceed to abolish the eight other boundaries. The family boundary is detrimental to the doctrine of universal love, while the sex-boundary and class-boundary are detrimental to the principle of equality. And the injuries due to race-boundary form the great obstacle in the way of universal love and complete equality. Consequently, these four boundaries would have to be abolished to usher in the Age of *Ta-t'ung* and Great Peace.

The next boundary to be abolished involves "occupation-boundary" which he links with the desire for personal wealth. He took up the idea from the *Li Yün* of "not keeping wealth for personal use" and "not exerting strength for personal benefit." Then he developed these ideas into principles of public ownership in agriculture, industry, commerce, the means of production. In fact, all these enterprises he said must be conducted in the future for the sole purpose of public welfare without private gain.

These boundaries having been abolished, the disappearance of the remaining three boundaries becomes only a matter of time. The abolition of disorder-boundary is to institute a government of Great Peace and to unite humanity in a single civilization. Then the abolition of kind-boundary is to extend love to all sentient beings. Finally, the abolition of suffering-boundary is to attain utmost happiness. Thus mankind will achieve the Age of Great Peace and the realm of *Ta-t'ung*, the prophecy of Confucius, the dream of K'ang Yu-wei.

Confucianism and Communism

The period from the end of the nineteenth century to the establishment of the Communism of 1949 was an age of great social disturbance, political instability and intellectual anarchy. The age tended toward skepticism and destructiveness. All established institutions, marriage, the family, society, the state, the law, came in for destructive criticism.

The collapse of the old dynastic system in 1911 and the failure of Confucian-garbed monarchical restoration in 1916 meant that, politically, Confucianism was almost dead. The man who led the open assault on Confucianism was Ch'en Tu-hsiu (1879–1942), founder of the Chinese Communist Party. For him, Confucianism meant only reaction and obscurantism. Together with Hu Shih (1891–1962) and other young Chinese scholars trained in the West, they started a New Culture Movement to destroy what remained of traditional Confucian culture and to replace it with Western ideologies of "science" and "democracy."

On the other hand, it would be a great mistake to consider the revolt against or hostility toward Confucianism, with its institutions and its values, as tantamount to the extermination of Confucianism. No Chinese political leaders would ever intend this; they would be much too intelligent to attempt to abandon Chinese cultural tradition and to scrap every vestige of the oldest civilization of the world.

For example, the Chinese Nationalist leader, Sun Yat-sen (1866–1925) was himself very much like K'ang Yu-wei and advocated the ideal of *Ta-t'ung*, although these two men differed in their interpretation and argued with each other for a long time about how China could best be preserved and served. Sun Yat-sen, in his first lecture on the *Principle of the People's Livelihood (Min Sheng Chu I)* wrote: "I propose today a definition for *Min shen* (People's Livelihood). It denotes the livelihood of the people, the existence of society, the welfare of the nation, the life of the masses. And now I shall use the phrase *Min Sheng* to describe one of the greatest problems that emerged in the West during the past century or more, and that is the social problem. Therefore, the *Principle of the People's Livelihood* is socialism, also known as Communism, and that is the doctrine of *Ta-t'ung*." [3] In other words, the doctrine of *Ta-t'ung* is the ideal of *Min-sheng;* the Principle of *Min-sheng* is the practice of *Ta-t'ung*. Hence the distinction between *Ta-t'ung* and *Min-sheng* is very slight; the Confucianist aspiration was already "socialism" before the word was invented. Now Confucianism and Communism alike, along with Capitalism and other systems, promise the brotherhood of man and the federation of the world.

In 1952, Sun Yat-sen's disciple Chiang Kai-shek (1886–) wrote and published a booklet in Taipei. In it Chiang again takes up the ideal of *Ta-tung* and elaborates the passage in the *Li Chi* into economic, social and political systems of *Ta-t'ung*.[4] In 1966 under Chiang's auspices, a "cultural renaissance" movement began in Taiwan to preserve Confucian tradition and ethics. By 1967 the Chinese government in Taiwan had officially created a Council for the Promotion of the Chinese Cultural Renaissance Movement, including the adoption of a "Code of Conduct for Youth." Its first commandment was "Be loyal to the national leader; a patriot of the nation; faithful and obedient to parents; respectful to teachers and the aged; and kindly and helpful to the poor and distressed." To Westerners this sounds like the Boy Scouts. To the Chinese it sounds like Confucianism.

There are other codes adopted by the Council including "good habits" and "good table manners," as well as laws forbidding smoking, drinking, and gambling. In addition, there are many activities promoted such as the development of new literary and art movements based upon ethics, democracy and science; development of tourism in order to help preserve historic sites and relics; planning and constructing stadiums, art galleries, music halls and other cultural facilities; inculcating good morals and customs through the use of mass communication media; and vigorously promoting a "New Life Movement" to modernize and rationalize life under the influence of the Confucian eight virtues. In fact, the government was to set standards for rites and music, social etiquette and correct dress so as to improve the Chinese image.

On the mainland of China under Communism, however, all the external appurtenances of the Confucian cult have disappeared, except perhaps a few Confucian temples used as historical museums as well as the temple and tomb of Confucius at Ch'u-fu, which was refurbished and preserved.

Although there has been a long tradition of hostility toward established religion in Communist China, Confucian tradition is still invoked in support of Communist ideology. In fact, in his early days Mao Tse-tung, Chairman of the Communist Party in China, was fundamentally under the influence of two Confucian scholars, K'ang Yu-wei and Liang Ch'i-ch'ao. This is what Mao wrote in his autobiography:

> I began studying in a local primary school when I was eight and remained there until I was thirteen years old . . . [Later] I went to the [new] school with my cousin [in Hsiang Hsiang, where his mother's family lived]. . . . I made good progress at this school. The teachers liked me, especially those who taught the classics because I wrote good essays in the classical manner. But my mind was not on the classics. I was reading

two books sent to me by my cousin, telling of the Reform Movement of K'ang Yu-wei, edited by Liang Ch'i-ch'ao. I read and reread these until I knew them by heart. I worshipped K'ang Yu-wei and Liang Ch'i-ch'ao and was very grateful to my cousin. . . .[5]

An examination of Mao Tse-tung's own writings, particularly his *On Practice* and *On New Democracy*,[6] reveals that he retains two elements of Confucianism in particular, consciousness of the problem of the relation between knowledge and conduct, and the ideal of *Ta-t'ung* (which Mao identifies with Communism).

In *On Practice*, for example, Mao Tse-tung contends that theory is no good in itself but must be applied in practice, as part of an effort not only to "acquire knowledge" but "to change reality." According to Mao, Marxism as a "science of history" when put into practice must become ethics, a philosophy of life; as a result, self-criticism is a necessary part of discipline for this purpose. Now it happens that Communist self-criticism is in some degree reminiscent of the Confucian doctrine of self-cultivation as elaborated by Wang Yang-ming.

In the view of Wang Yang-ming, "knowledge is the beginning of conduct; conduct is the completion of knowledge."[7] Hence Wang Yang-ming urged self-cultivation as a process by which the true philosopher can bring his thought and conduct into consonance, so that knowledge is realized in action and action contributes to knowledge. This idea has been clearly echoed by Mao Tse-tung.

It is difficult to explain Mao Tse-tung's failure to give credit to Wang Yang-ming, although he often blends Communist ideas with the local traditions. As Mao wrote, "we must make a summing-up from Confucius down to Sun Yat-sen and inherit this precious legacy."[8] Perhaps in Mao's desire to dissociate his ideology from the past, he finds it necessary not to lay too much stress on any indebtedness to Confucianism.

Since the beginning of the Great Proletarian Cultural Revolution in the middle of 1966, there is a strong tendency to replace Confucianism with Maoism (or the thought of Mao Tse-tung) in China. However, the two major areas of concern of Maoism are still very much like the Confucianism of the past. One concern is for values; the other for reality.

For example, in Maoism, happiness means the relatively secure possession of the minimum necessities for decent life and the absence of suffering from deprivation, oppression, exploitation and neglect. These have also been the cardinal aims of Confucianism.

Another illustration is Mao's concept of righteousness, which centers around personal selflessness. An article entitled "Liang Chen-yu, A Good Cadre Reared on Mao Tse-tung's Thought" gave the following description:

> After a rainstorm on July 29, 1966, the Shihtouyu River in Lonan County was in full spate. Mountain torrents poured into it carrying silt and rocks down with them.
>
> At that moment Yin Yung-shan, a yonng peasant, reached the river bank bound for a village on the other side with an important message concerning arrangements for carrying on the great proletarian cultural revolution. Liang saw how dangerous it was to cross. Reminded of Chairman Mao's great teaching: "He should be more concerned about the Party and the masses than about any individual, and more concerned about others than about himself. Only thus can he be considered a Communist," Liang hurried down to the river to help Yin Yung-shan wade across.
>
> Just as they reached mid-stream, a big wave threw both of them off their feet. . . . As they were swept near a deep pool where the water was less turbulent, Liang used all his strength to push Yin Yung-shan out of the swift current and so helped Yin reach the river bank. But he himself was carried down river by the flood. . . .
>
> Among Liang's belongings were found that revolutionary treasure—the four volumes of Selected Works of Mao Tse-tung and a dozen diaries dating from 1948 to 1966. These diaries record his glorious life of boundless loyalty to Chairman Mao, the people and the Party. . . .[9]

As one can see, even if the Cultural Revolution on the surface has put an end to the earlier policy of preserving the Confucian heritage, this does not mean a total negation of the Confucian principles. In the revaluation of Confucian tradition, the Communists have rejected much, but at the same time they have also made much use of Confucian ethics and traditional literature to elucidate Marxist doctrines. As time goes on, many desirable elements of Confucianism that have been called feudal and reactionary will be assured of preservation in human memory, for Confucius was one of the greatest thinkers of all time and his teachings, however, modified and adapted to changing circumstances down the centuries, are precious and indestructible.

FOOTNOTES

For all Chapters

INTRODUCTION

1. *Shuo-wen chieh-tzu,* or *Explanation of Words and Elucidation of Characters,* by *Hsu Shen, fl.* A.D. 100., the earliest Chinese dictionary.

2. cf. "The Master said: 'Chou had the advantage of surveying the two preceding dynasties (Hsia and Shang). How replete is its culture! I follow Chou'" (*Lun Yü,* III–4).

3. It preaches the right of the superior to rule and the duty of the inferior to obey and be content with his lot.

4. *Chu Wen-kung wen-chi* (Works of Master Chu), ch. 36 "Reply to Ch'en T'ung-fu".

5. Lin Yutang: *My Country and My People,* p. 100.

6. Wing-tsi Chan, "Modern Trends in Chinese Philosophy and Religion," *Modern Trends in World Religions,* p. 216.

7. cf. Fung Yu-lan, *A Short History of Chinese Philosophy,* edited by Derk Bodde, p. 8.

8. In the *Li Chi,* there is also a chapter on music, which may have been taken from *Hsün Tzu.*

9. The year 628 B.C. is the date assigned to the latest document.

CHAPTER *1*

1. The term *Shang Ti* was adopted by Protestant missionaries to translate the name of the Christian God.

2. Tung Tso-pin's "An Interpretation of the Ancient Chinese Civilization," p. 18.

3. *Ibid.*

4. *Ibid.* p. 19.

5. *Ibid.*

6. p. 19. Oracle bones, being produced exclusively for the king and the ruling house, tell us nothing of anyone else.

7. For instance, the Chou house was believed to be descended from an ancestor called Hou Chi, or "Millet Ruler," who was deified as an agricultural deity. From time to time, the list of local deities might be revised by striking out those who were thought fit to be removed and filling up the vacancies by the deification of those more recently deceased.

8. *Li Chi*, Bk XXIX *"Piao Ki"* ("The Record of Example"). See Legge, trans. & edited by Chais, *Li Ki*, vol. II, p. 342. *Li Chi* in its present form is a compilation made in the Han dynasty from various texts.

9. The earliest anthology of Chinese poetry; see Introduction.

10. T'ang was the founder of the Shang (Yin) dynasty.

11. See Introduction.

12. Duke Chou (d. 1094 B.C.), a regent to King Ch'eng (r.1104–1068), was a warrior and a great statesman. Many documents of the *Shu Ching* were traditionally attributed to his authorship.

13. This was presumed to be composed by Duke Chou to dissuade Prince Shih (also called Duke Chao, d. 1056 B.C.) from retiring as the chief minister to Ch'eng.

14. This was attributed to Tsu Ch'iu-ming in the latter part of the 5th century B.C. But modern scholarship holds that it was written or compiled around 4th century. Also see Introduction.

15. A collection of historical discourses, arranged under states, and covering about the same period as does the *Tso Chuan*—from 722 to 481 B.C.

16. In the *Hsün Tzu* there are chapters on rites and music. Most of the chapters of the *Li Chi* are generally be-

lieved to have been written by the followers of Hsün Tzu (active between 298 and 238 B.C.).

CHAPTER 2

1. As to the difference between *jen* (human-heartedness) and *yi* (righteousness), Mencius said: "Human-heartedness represents the human heart; righteousness, the human way" (The *Meng Tzu* Bk. VI-A). Generally speaking, *jen* implies righteousness; a *jen* action is certainly righteous, but an action to be righteous does not necessarily mean that it is a *jen* action.

2. The Chinese word *Ming* has been variously translated as "Fate," "Destiny" or "Decree." To Confucius, it might mean the Decree of Heaven or *T'ien Ming*, as he said: "At fifty, I knew the Decree of Heaven" (II–4). In later Confucianism, the word comes to mean those aspects of existence which are beyond human control.

3. Taoists, also known as naturalists, were men who withdrew from the world, regarding nature as their retreat and simply living their life ideal. *Wu-wei* (doing nothing contrary to Nature) is the essence of their doctrine. This is the naturalistic line of thought known as Taoism, which is based on the exaltation of *Tao* and idealization of nature, as illustrated in the *Tao Te Ching*, traditionally attributed to Lao Tzu, an elder contemporary of Confucius.

4. The word "*tao*," as Confucius used it, denotes the moral principle, particularly the proper way of living.

5. cf. Fung Yu-lan: *A Short History of Chinese Philosophy*, edited by Derk Boode, p. 45.

6. In the *Lun Yü*, Tzu Lu spoke for Confucius about his persistent, if not frustrating, effort: "The superior man serves in the government because it is his duty to do so. The fact that he is bound to fail, he knows already" (XVIII–7).

7. In the *Lun Yü* we read: "Tzu Hsia said: I have heard [from Confucius] this saying: 'Death and life are as decreed; wealth and honor depend upon Heaven'" (XII–5).

8. The Chinese word *li* has been translated by a variety of terms, including "ceremonial," "ritual," and "rules of propriety." As a matter of fact, the English language

and Occidental thought seem alike incapable of supply-
ing a term that can express its full meaning. Although
we translate it as "a code of rituals" or "rules of propriety," it really means much more than that. We resort
to a quotation from a French scholar, J. M.
Callery:
"*Li* epitomizes the entire Chinese mind. . . . Its affec-
tions, if it has any, are satisfied by *li;* its duties are fulfilled by *li;* its virtues and vices are referred to *li;* the
natural relations of created beings essentially link themselves to *li.*" (trans. from *Mémoire des Rites,* p. XVI)
This statement serves to show the comprehensiveness of
the Chinese word *li.* Ancient ceremonies were of many
kinds and grades. The *Li Chi,* or the *Book of Rites,*
gives detailed instructions on how to properly perform
these ceremonies. Many of these ceremonies we regard
as factitious and extravagant. In justifying them, Confucian scholars gave them new interpretations and read
into them ethical ideas. Let us take, for example, the
mourning and sacrificial ceremonies, designed primarily
for the feudal aristocrats, who could afford these elaborate and costly performances. But in their defense of
these ceremonies, Confucian scholars made their appeal
to men's emotion. These ceremonial practices, such as
"mourning garments, a rush staff, living in a hovel, eat-
ing rice gruel, using firewood for mat and clods for a
pillow," they argued, were originally "the expression of
men's deepest sorrow and affectionate yearning for the
dead," "the calling up of memories and intentions, of
thought and longings." In their opinion, all sacramental
acts, therefore, should be performed in their proper
form, in order to pay respect to the departed and
regulate the emotions of the living. Seen in this light,
they had provided an ethical justification for these ritual
observances. For further illustrations, read Ch'u Chai's
introduction in the *Li Chi,* trans. by James Legge.

9. *cf.* H. G. Creel: *Confucius and the Chinese Way,* p. 86.

10. By "genuine nature," we mean what is true in one's
    nature; it is incompatible with any artificiality or false-
    hood.

CHAPTER *3*

1. Mo Tzu flourished 468?–390? B.C. We have little in-
    formation of Yang Chu, except one chapter of the *Lieh
    Tzu,* entitled "Yang Chu," attributed to a Neo-Taoist
    writer of the third century A.D.

To Mencius, Yang Chu, who held the principle of "each one for himself," and Mo Tzu, who advocated the principle of "all-embracing love," were both extremists who failed to attain the golden mean, and who therefore perverted the true way. See the *Meng Tzu* VIIA-26. Moreover, he did not take kindly to those philosophers, who professed allegiance to the teachings of Shen Nung, the Divine Farmer, known as the "agricultural school," who believed in the simple life even to the extent of having a sovereign labor in the field for his own food. See ibid., IIIA-4; III8-9; VI8-1.

2. In the *Lun Yü*, Confucius said: "The superior man takes *yi* as his basic stuff [*chih*] and performs it according to *li*" (XV,17). See passages II-24; IV-16; XIII-3,6.

3. The size of the ancient *li* is not known; the modern *li* is about one-third of a mile.

4. The size of the ancient *mou* is not known; the modern *mou* is about one-third of an acre.

5. *Chien* means "well," and *t'ien* means "field." If *chien* is put within a square, it will form a field divided into nine equal squares. The central lot is the public field, being cultivated jointly by the eight households.

    chien   *t'ien*   *chien* within the square

6. See the *Lun Yü*, XIII-9.

CHAPTER **4**

1. See the *Shih Chi*, ch. 74.

2. According to William James, philosophers may be divided into two groups—the tender-minded and the tough-minded. See his *Pluralistic Universe*.

3. The Three Kings were the founders of the three dynasties, King Yü of Hsia, King T'ang of Shang, and King Wen of Chou.

4. This was an offshoot of the Taoists, who taught a theory that each period of history was determined by one of the five elements: earth, wood, metal, fire, and water. It was also known as the Yin-yang school, believing in the existence of *yin* and *yang* as two cosmic

principles, through whose reactions all creation was effected.

5. See Y. P. Mei's "Hsün Tzu's Theory of Education," *Tsing Hua Journal of Chinese Studies*, New Series II, Number 2 (June 1961), p. 365.

6. To Hsün Tzu, *li* denotes something very important and fundamental in social communications. In Chapter 19, he stressed that the value of *li*, aside from serving to counteract the evil of human nature, lies in its use to beautify and refine the expression of human emotion.

7. Mo Tzu, see note 1 (p. 00) in ch. 3.

8. Hui Tzu, also known as Hui Shih, a fourth-third century B.C. philosopher of the Ming-chia (School of Names).

9. Chuang Tzu, fl. 369–286 B.C., also known as Chuang Chou, the most brilliant of the early Taoist philosophers.

CHAPTER 6

1. The *yin-yang* doctrine, which began its rise in the 4th century B.C., as an offshoot of the Taoist school, believes in the existence of *yin* (female or negative) and *yang* (male or positive) as the two cosmic principles in whose interaction all changes in the universe were produced.

2. This important work is also known as the *Kung-yang Chuan* (*Kung-yang Commentary*). See Introduction p. 18.

CHAPTER 7

7. The Neo-Confucian concept of *Li*, the metaphysical principle, should not be confused with the Confucian *li* meaning "rite or ceremony." The two characters, though pronounced identically, are quite different.

CHAPTER 8

1. For the list of Chu Hsi's works, see Carson Chang: *The Development of Neo-Confucian Thought* (1957), Ch. 12.

2. See Fung Yu-lan, *History of Chinese Philosophy*, trans. by Derk Bodde, Vol. II, Ch. XIV, p. 578.

3. In the *Ch'uan-hsi lu*, "The Teacher further said: 'The word *ko* in *ko wu* is the same as the *ko* in Mencius' saying that 'a great man may rectify (*ko*) the mind of his soverign' (the *Meng Tzu* IVA–20).' "

4. Edwin D. Reischauer & J. K. Fairbank: *EAST ASIA: THE GREAT TRADITION*, Ch. 8, p. 309.

CHAPTER 9

1. Quoted from *K'ang Tzu-pien Nien-p'u* (Autobiographical Chronology) in Winberg Chai, *The Political Thought of K'ang Yu-wei: A Study of its Origin and Its Influence*, Ph.D. thesis, New York University, p. 3.

2. Quoted in Winberg Chai, *The Political Thought of K'ang Yu-wei, op. cit.*

3. Sun Yat-sen, *San Min Chu I* (Taipei, International Book Co.), 1953 edition, page _____.

4. Chiang Kai-shek, *Chapters on National Fecundity, Social Welfare, Education and Health and Happiness*, Taipei edition, 1953.

5. Edgar Snow, *Red Star Over China* (New York, Random House, 1938), pp. 128–133; *The Autobiography of Mao Tse-tung* (Canton, China, Truth Book Co., 1938, revised in 1949), p. 11.

6. See Winberg Chai (ed.), *Essential Works of Chinese Communism* (New York, Bantam Books, 1969).

7. Feng Yu-lan, *History of Chinese Philosophy* (Princeton, Princeton University Press), Vol. II, 1953, p. 604.

8. Quoted in Shen-yu Dai, "The Roots of Chinese Ideology," *Current History* (September, 1963), p. 159.

9. *Peking Review* (March 15, 1963), p. 19.

Glossary

Translation of technical philosophical terms is extremely difficult, for a single Chinese character often condenses the meaning of many English words. Moreover, many philosophical ideas are difficult in themselves, however lucidly translated and interpreted. For added clarity, a selective glossary is included here.

CH'AN (Japanese *zen*) or CH'AN-NA (Sanskrit *dhyāna*). Meditation, contemplation—originally, the word for instaneous intuition of truth.

CH'ENG. Sincerity, truthfulness, realness—being one's true or real self.

CHENG MING. Rectification of names—a Confucian doctrine holding that names should correspond to actualities.

CH'I. Life breath, vital force, matter-energy, *i.e.*, whatever is within the realm of matter, opposed to *li*, eternal principle or law of nature underlying a thing.

CH'IEN. A trigram and hexagram, symbolic of heaven, male, strength, creativity, etc.

CHIEN AI. A Mohist concept of "all-embracing love" or universal love, *i.e.*, love for all, equally and without discrimination, opposed to the Confucian concept of love with gradation.

CHIH CHIH. Extension of knowledge.

CHING. Seriousness, attentiveness, prudence.

CHING. Quiescence.

CH'ING. Emotions, feelings.

CHING T'IEN. Well-field (system).

CHÜN TZU. Lond's son, princely men—originally, noble overlord and later, perfect gentleman or superior man.

CHUNG SHU. Conscientiousness and altruism, *i.e.*, faithfulness to one's self and consideration for the feeling of others.

CHUNG YUNG. *The Doctrine of the Mean.*

FA. Law, model; in the Legalist school, it involves the concepts of law, strategy and power.

FA CHIA. The Legalist school, Legalism.

HAN HSÜEH. Han Learning.

HSIAO JEN. Little fellow, common man—originally, a peasant and later, a mean, despicable person.

HSIAO K'ANG. Minor peace, small tranquility.

HSIAO TI. Filial piety and fraternal love.

HSIN HSÜEH. Learning or Study of the Mind, referring to the Idealist Neo-Confucianism.

HSING. Human nature.

HSING. Form, shape.

HSING ERH HSIA. "What is below shape," *i.e.*, what is physical.

HSING ERH SHANG. "What is above shape," *i.e.*, what is metaphysical.

HSING LI HSÜEH. Learning or Study of the Nature and Principle, *i.e.*, Neo-Confucianism of the Sung and Ming Periods.

HSÜAN HSÜEH. Mysterious Learning, *i.e.*, Taoist metaphysics.

JEN. Humanity, human-heartedness, benevolence.

JEN LUN. Human relationships (see *wu lun*).

JU. Literati, scholars, men who helped with expert advice on ceremonials (*li*), and later, identified with Confucians.

JU CHIA. Confucian school, Confucianism.

KO WU. Investigation of things.

K'UN. A trigram and hexagram, symbolic of earth, female, weakness, etc.

LI. Profit, advantageous gain, contrary to what is righteous (see *yi*).

LI. Ceremonies, rites, propriety, code of proper conduct, rules of social conduct.

LI. Principle, reason (see *ch'i*).

LI HSÜEH. Learning or Study of Principle, referring to the Rationalist Neo-Confucianism.

LIANG CHIH. Intuitive (innate) knowledge.

LIANG NENG. Intuitive ability.

MING. Decree, fate, destiny.

MING. Name (see *cheng ming*).

MING CHIA. School of Names, *i.e.*, Sophists, Logicians, Dialecticians.

MING CHIAO. Morals and institutions, literally, "religion of names."

MING FEN. Nominal status, social status.

MING SHIH. Names and actualities.

MO CHIA. Mohist school, Mohism, based on the teachings of Mo Tzu (fl. 479–381 B.C.).

PA TAO. The way of a feudal leader or a tyrant, contrary to the "kingly way." (see *wang tao*).

PA KUI. Eight trigrams.

SHANG TI. The Lord on High, Supreme Emperor, God.

SHE CHI. (Spirits of) land and grains.

SHENG JEN. Sage.

SHENG WANG. Sage-king.

SHIH CHUNG. Timely mean, *i.e.*, a relative mean in human affairs.

TA HSÜEH. *The Great Learning.*

TA T'UNG. Great unity.

T'AI CHI. Supreme Ultimate, Great Ultimate.

T'AI HSU. Great Void.

T'AI HO. Great HARMONY.

TAO. The Way, the principle, the truth, the cosmic order. The Confucian *tao* is ethical and deals with the way of life, while the Taoist *Tao* is essentially metaphysical and can be taken as an all-embracing first principle of the universe.

TAO CHIA OR TAO TE CHIA. Taoist school, Taoism.

TAO HSÜEH. Learning or Study of the *Tao*, referring to Neo-Confucianism.

TAO T'UNG. Line of succession of the *Tao*, *i.e.*, a theory first formulated by the Confucian scholar Han Yü (768–824) of the T'ang dynasty.

TE. Virtue (Confucian), the Power inherent in a thing (Taoist).

TI. The Lord, God, the Emperor.

T'IEN. Heaven, both in the physical and supernatural senses (Confucian), Nature (Taoist).

T'IEN KUAN. Natural senses.

T'IEN LI. Heavenly reason, divine law, the moral principle of Heaven.

T'IEN MING. Mandate of Heaven.

T'IEN TAO. Way of Heaven.

T'IEN TI. Heaven-and-Earth, the universe.

WANG TAO. Kingly way that embodies virtuous government, opposite of "the way of a tyrant" (see *pa tao*).

WU HSING. Five Elements (water, fire, wood, metal and earth), a fantastic theory interpreting the structure of the universe (see *Yin-yang* school).

WU LUN. Five cardinal human relationships between king and subject, between father and son, between husband and wife, between brothers, between friends.

WU WEI. Non-action, inactivity, non-assertion—refraining from activity contrary to Nature.

YI. Righteousness—what one ought to do, as opposed to what one would like to do for profit (see *li*).

YI LI CHIH HSÜEH. Learning or Study of the basic principles.

YIN YANG. The *Yin* and the *Yang* are the basic polar dicholomies of Chinese thinking, representing two cosmic principles or forces, the negative (female) and the positive (male), always contrasting but complementary. Chinese cosmology is based on the *Yin Yang* doctrine, comparable to the mascule-feminine principle of the ancient Egyptians.

YIN YANG CHIA. The *Yin Yang* school, an offshoot of the Taoist, based on the two cosmic principles of Yin and Yang whose reactions created all things. Tsou Yen (340–260 B.C.?) is often referred to as the leading thinker of this school. It was also called the *Wu Hsing* school, teaching the theory that each period of history was dominated by one of the five elements.

YÜ CHOW. Heaven-and-Earth, the universe.

YÜAN. Origin or source (of history and human affairs).

Selective Bibliography

GENERAL WORKS ON CHINESE RELIGION AND PHILOSOPHY

Chai, Ch'u and Winberg. *The Story of Chinese Philosophy.* New York: Washington Square Press, Inc., 1961.

———. *Essential Works of Confucianism.* New York: Bantam Books, 1965; (hardcover) University Books, 1965.

Chai, Ch'u. "Chinese Humanism: A Study of Chinese Mentality and Temperament," *Social Research*, 26 (1959), 31–46.

Chan, Wing-tsit. *An Outline and an Annotated Bibliography of Chinese Philosophy.* New Haven: Far Eastern Publications, 1961.

———. *A Source Book in Chinese Philosophy.* New Jersey: Princeton University Press, 1963.

Chan, Wing-tsit et al. *The Great Asian Religions.* New York: The Macmillan Co., 1969.

Creel, H. G. *Chinese Thought: From Confucius to Mao Tse-tung.* Chicago: University of Chicago Press, 1953.

Day, Clarence Burton. *The Philosophers of China, Classical and Contemporary.* New York: Philosophical Library, 1962.

de Bary, Wm. Theodore et al. *Sources of Chinese Tradition.* New York: Columbia University Press, 1960.

Fung Yu-lan. *A History of Chinese Philosophy*, 2 vols., trans. by Derk Bodde. New Jersey: Princeton University Press, 1952–1953.

———. *A Short History of Chinese Philosophy.* New York: Macmillan Co., 1948.

———. *The Spirit of Chinese Philosophy*, trans. by E. R. Hughes. London: Kelgan Paul, 1947; (paperback) Boston: Beacon Press, 1962.

Hu Shih. "The Establishment of Confucianism as a State Religion during the Han Dynasty," *Journal of the North China Branch of the Royal Asiatic Society*, 60 (1929), 20–41.

―――. "Religion and Philosophy in Chinese History," *Symposium on Chinese Culture* (Shanghai, 1931), 31–58.

Hughes, E. R. *Chinese Philosophy in Classical Times*. London: J. M. Dent & Sons, 1942; rev. ed., 1954.

Lin Yutang. *The Wisdom of China and India*. New York: Random House, 1942.

Liu, Wu-chi. *A Short History of Confucian Philosophy*. Baltimore: Penguin Books (paperback), 1955.

Moore, Charles A., ed. *Essays in East-West Philosophy*. Honolulu: University of Hawaii Press, 1951.

―――. *Philosophy East and West*. New Jersey: Princeton University Press, 1964.

Needham, Joseph. *Science and Civilization in China*, vol. 2. Cambridge: Cambridge University Press, 1956.

Thompson, Laurence G. *Chinese Religion: An Introduction*. Belmont, California: Dickenson Publishing Co., 1969.

Wright, Arthur F., ed. *Studies in Chinese Thought*. Chicago: The University of Chicago Press, 1953.

―――, ed. *Confucianism and Chinese Civilization*. New York: Atheneum, 1964.

James Legge's Translation of *The Chinese Classics*
With the assistance of the eminent Chinese scholar, Wang T'ao (1828–1897), James Legge translated the *Four Books* and the *Five Classics* in seven volumes:

Vol. I. *Confucian Analects, The Great Learning*, and *The of the Mean*
Vol. II. *The Works of Mencius*
Vol. III. *The Book of History (Shu Ching)*
Vol. IV. *The Book of Odes (Shih Ching)*
Vol. V. *Ch'un Ch'iu* with *The Tso Chuan*
Vol. VI. *The Book of Changes (I Ching)*
Vol. VII. *The Book of Ritual (Li Chi)*

The first five volumes were published in Hong Kong in 1861, 1865, 1871, and 1872, with Chinese text and full commentary, while the last two volumes, without Chinese text or extensive commentary, were published in 1882 and 1885 in the Sacred Books of the East Series edited by Friedrich Max Müller. The first five volumes listed above were recently reprinted by Oxford University Press, and the last two, edited by Ch'u Chai and Winberg Chai, with introduction and study guide, were reprinted by University Books, Inc., New York, 1964 and 1967.

WORKS ON CONFUCIUS

Chang Chi-yün. *Life of Confucius,* translated by Shih Chao-yin. Taiwan: China Culture Publishing Foundation, 1954.

Confucius. *The Wisdom of Confucius,* ed. and trans. by Lin Yutang. New York: The Modern Library, 1938.

———. *Confucian Analects,* trans. by Ezra Pound. London: 1956.

———. *The Analects of Confucius,* translated by Wm. E. Sooth. London: 1937.

———. *The Analects of Confucius,* translated by Arthur Waley. London: 1938.

———. *The Best of Confucius,* trans. by James R. Ware. Garden City: Halcyon House, 1950; (paperback), *The Sayings of Confucius.* New York: New American Library.

Creel, H. G. *Confucius, the Man and the Myth.* New York: John Day Company, 1940; (paperback), *Confucius and the Chinese Way.* New York: Harper and Brothers, 1960.

Dubs, Homer H. "Confucius: "His Life and Teaching," *Philosophy,* 26 (1951), 30–36.

Liu, Wu-chi. *Confucius, His Life and Time.* New York: Philosophical Library, 1956.

Yetts, W. Percival. *The Legend of Confucius.* London: The Chinese Society, 1943.

WORKS ON MENCIUS

Chen, Ta-tsi. "Mencius' Theory on Righteousness and Profit," *Chinese Culture*, 1, no. 1 (1957), 20–54.

Lau, D. C. "Theories of Human Nature in Mencius and Shyuntzyy [Hsüntzu]," *Bulletin of the School of Oriental and African Studies*, 15 (1953), 541–565.

Mencius. *The Book of Mencius*, trans. by Lionel Giles. London: John Murray, 1942.

————. *The Sayings of Mencius*, trans. by James R. Ware. New York: New American Library, 1960.

Richards, I. A. *Mencius on the Mind: Experiments in Multiple Definition*. London: Kegan Paul, 1932.

Waley, Arthur. *Three Ways of Thought in Ancient China*. London: Allen and Unwin, 1939; (paperback) New York: Doubleday, 1956.

Wei, Francis C. *The Political Principles of Mencius*. Shanghai: Presbyterian Mission Press, 1916.

Wu, John C. H. "Mencius' Philosophy of Human Nature and Natural Law," *Chinese Culture*, 1, no. 1 (1957), 1–19.

WORKS ON HSÜN TZU

Cheng, Andrew Chih-yi. *Hsüntzu's Theory of Human Nature and Its Influence on Chinese Thought*. Peking: Privately published, 1926.

Dubs, Homer H. *Hsüntzu, the Moulder of Ancient Confucianism*. London: Arthur Probsthain, 1927.

Duyvendak, J. J. L. "The Chronology of Hsüntzu," *T'oung Pao*, 26 (1929), 73–95.

Hsün Tzu. *The Works of Hsuntze*, trans. by H. H. Dubs. London: Arthur Probsthain, 1928.

————. *Hsün Tzu: Basic Writings,* trans. by Burton Watson. New York: Columbia University Press, 1963.

Mei, Y. P. "Hsün Tzu's Theory of Education, with an English Translation of the *Hsün Tzu,* Chapter I, An Exhortation to Learning," *Tsing Hua Journal of Chinese Studies,* new series II, no. 2 (1961), 361–379.

WORKS ON TA HSÜEH (GREAT LEARNING) AND CHUNG YUNG
(DOCTRINE OF THE MEAN)

Ta hsüeh. "The Great Learning," trans. by E. R. Hughes, in his *The Great Learning and the Man-in-Action.* New York: Dutton, 1943.

————. "The Great Learning," trans. by Lin Yutang, in his *The Wisdom of Confucius.*

————. *Confucius: The Great Digest and Unwebbing Pivot,* trans. by Ezra Pound. New York: New Directions, 1951.

Chung yung. "Central Harmony," trans. by Ku Hung Ming, in Lin Yutant's *The Wisdom of Confucius.*

————. "The Man-in-action," trans. by E. R. Hughes, in his *The Great Learning and the Man-in-Action.*

WORKS ON TUNG CHUNG-SHU

Yao, Shan-yu. "The Cosmological and Inthropological Philosophy of Tung Chung-shu," *Journal of the North China Branch of Royal Asiatic Society,* 73 (1948), 40–68.

WORKS ON NEO-CONFUCIANISM

Bruce, J. Percy. *Chu Hsi and His Masters.* London: Arthur Probsthain, 1923.

Cady, Lyman Van Law. *The Philosophy of Lu Hsiang-shan, A Neo-Confucian Monistic Idealist,* typescript, 2 vols. New York: Union Theological Seminary, 1939.

Chai, Ch'u. "Neo-Confucianism of the Sung-Ming Periods," *Social Research*, 18, no. 3 (1951), 370–392.

Chan, Wing-tsit. "Neo-Confucianism and Chinese Scientific Thought," *Philosophy—East and West*, 6 (1957), 309–332.

Chang, Carsun. *The Development of Neo-Confucian Thought*. New York: Bookman Associates, 1957.

———. *Wang Yang-ming, the Idealist Philosophy of the Six-teenth-Century China*. New York: St. John's University Press, 1962.

Chu Hsi. *The Philosophy of Human Nature, by Chu Hsi*, trans. by J. Percy Bruce. London: Arthur Probsthain, 1922.

Graham, A. C. *Two Chinese Philosophers: Ch'eng Ming-tao and Ch'eng Yi-ch'uan*. London: Lund Humphries, 1958.

Hocking, W. E. "Chu Hsi's Theory of Knowledge," *Harvard Journal of Asiatic Studies*, 1 (1936), 109–127.

Huang, Siu-chi. *Lu Hsiang-shan, A Twelfth Century Chinese Idealist Philosopher*. New Haven: American Oriental Society, 1944.

Wang Yang-ming. *Instructions for Practical Living*, trans. by Wing-tsit Chan. New York: Columbia University Press, 1960.

———. *The Philosophy of Wang Yang-ming*, trans. by Frederick Goodrich Henke. Chicago: Open Court, 1916.

WORKS ON CONFUCIANISM IN MODERN CHINA

Briere, O. *Fifty Years of Chinese Philosophy, 1898–1950*, trans. by Laurence Thompson. London: Allen and Unwin, 1956.

Chai, Winberg. "The Political Thought of K'ang Yu-wei: A Study of Its Origin and Its Influence," unpublished Ph.D. dissertation, New York University, 1965.

Chan, Wing-tsit. "Modern Trends in Chinese Philosophy and Religion," Joseph M. Kitagawa, ed. *Modern Trends in World Religions*. Chicago: Open Court, 1959, 193–220.

Cheng, T'ien-hsi. *China moulded by Confucius, The Chinese Way in Western Light*. London: Stevens and Sons, 1946.

Dai, Shen-yu. *Mao Tse-tung and Confucianism*, typescript, University of Pennsylvania, 1952; microfilm, University of Michigan, 1953.

David, T. K. "Philosophy in Contemporary China," *Far Eastern Economic Review*, 23 (1957), 35–37.

Fung Yu-lan. "Philosophy in New China According to Fung Yu-lan," *East and West* (July, 1952), 105–107.

Hsiao, Kung-ch'uan. "K'ang Yu-wei and Confucianism," *Monumenta Serica*, 18 (1959), 96–212.

Hu Shih. *The Chinese Renaissance*. Chicago: University of Chicago Press, 1934.

Hummel, William F. "K'ang Yu-wei, Historical Critic and Social Philosopher, 1858–1927," *Pacific Historical Review*, 4 (1935), 343–355.

K'ang Yu-wei. *Ta T'ung Shu, The One-World Philosophy of K'ang Yu-wei*, trans. by Laurence G. Thompson, London: Allen and Unwin, 1958.

Liang Ch'i-ch'ao. *Intellectual Trends in the Ch'ing Period*, trans. by Immanuel C. Y. Hsü. Cambridge, Mass.: Harvard University Press, 1959.

Nivison, David S. "Communist Ethics and Chinese Tradition," *The Journal of Asian Studies*, 16 (1959), 51–74.

Rowbotham, Arnold H. "The Impact of Confucianism on Seventeeth Century Europe," *Far Eastern Quarterly*, 4 (1945), 224–242.

Index